Small Quilts

The Vanessa-Ann Collection

Oxmoor
House®

Designers

Trice Boerens
Miriam Gourley
Margaret Marti
Jo Packham
Julia Kirton Smith
Debbie C. Thurgood
Susan Whitelock
Terrece Woodruff

The photographs in this book were taken at the home of Pat and Clyde Buehler, Ogden, Utah; at The Washington School Inn and Snowed Inn, Park City, Utah; and at Trends and Traditions and Ivywood in Ogden, Utah. The Vanessa-Ann Collection wishes to express its appreciation to each for their trust and cooperation.

Book Division of Southern Progress Corporation
P.O. Box 2463, Birmingham, Alabama 35201

Library of Congress Catalog Number: 87-61720
ISBN: 0-8487-0735-4
Manufactured in the United States of America
Fourth Printing 1992

Executive Editor: Nancy J. Fitzpatrick
Production Manager: Jerry Higdon
Associate Production Manager: Rick Litton
Art Director: Bob Nance

Small Quilts

Editor: Charlotte Hagood
Editorial Assistant: Laura Miller Kurtz, Laurie Anne Pate
Copy Chief: Mary Jean Haddin
Designer: Melissa Jones Clark
Computer Artist: Rick Tucker
Photographer: Ryne Hazen

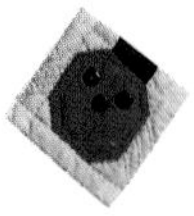

Contents

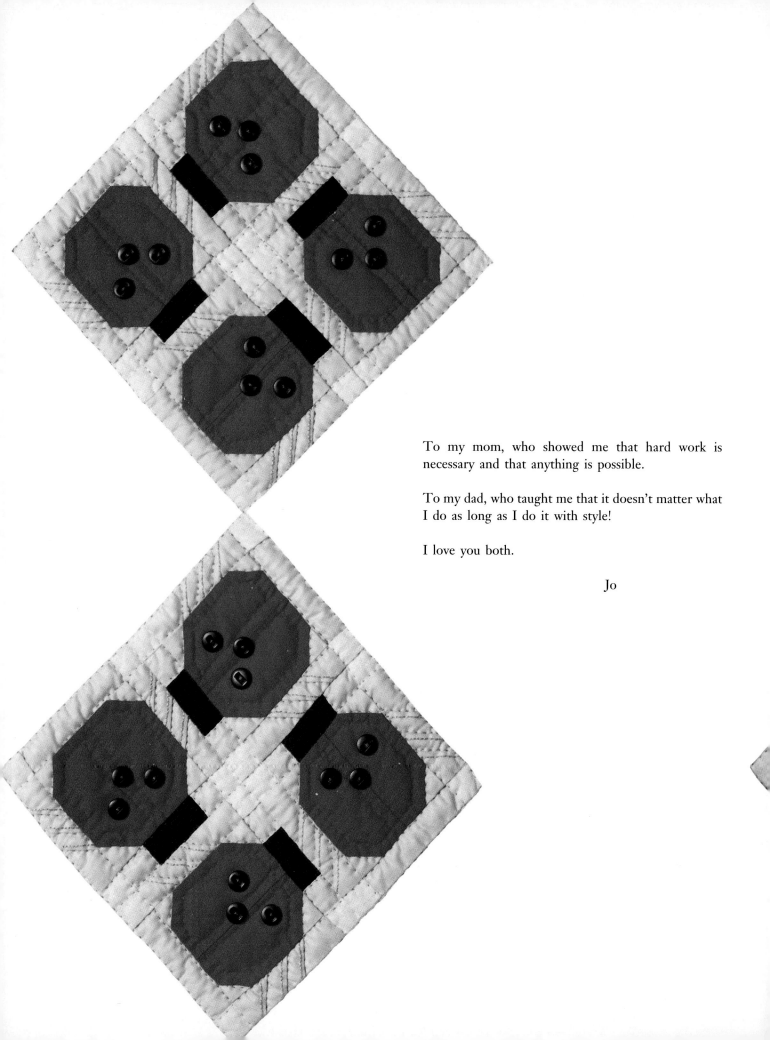

To my mom, who showed me that hard work is necessary and that anything is possible.

To my dad, who taught me that it doesn't matter what I do as long as I do it with style!

I love you both.

Jo

Friends...

One recent Saturday morning, I ducked into the fabric store near my house for a quick look. (I can never pass even a few bolts of fabric without stopping to inspect them.) On this trip, I was surprised to see an old acquaintance who, I had thought, rarely sews. Yet in her hands was a shiny, new quilt book. She was obviously selecting fabric and supplies for a new project.

I have known this woman for some fifteen years, and I feel sure she would agree with me that there is not an "artsy" bone in her body. Maybe not even a craftsy one. But this friend will somehow find time in a busy schedule to make the quilt that she can regard as her masterpiece. Making this quilt will satisfy the same emotional need that creating a beautiful painting does for the artist. And as she stitches, my friend will have the pleasure of seeing her talents, skills, and interests grow in unexpected ways.

Gone are the days when making a quilt was necessary to keep the baby warm or cover Grandmother's feather bed. Today we have the luxury of quilting just for the art of it, for the pure delight of playing with colors, textures, and shapes. *Small Quilts* is meant to open the imagination of the reader to the wonderful possibilities of combining fabric and buttons, colors and trims, to create small perfect works of art. These precious studies in fiber call for the traditional skills of piecing, appliqué, and sometimes a bit of embroidery. And for weaving our own interpretations of the quilter's art into the fabric with needle and thread.

Pick a favorite from the pages of this book. Regardless of your experience or skill, you can proceed with satisfaction, from the careful cutting of the pieces to the last stitch in the binding, producing quilted works that are imaginative and personal. Some of you will make a small quilt that is an exact and perfect copy of one in a photograph. Others will adapt the color and the trim of the quilts to match their own tastes. Perhaps a special quilt will become the springboard for your imagination, just as a familiar landscape inspires an artist over and over again to create many and varied works.

If, some Saturday morning, you find yourself with this volume in your hands in a fabric store near your home, let it liberate your imagination and free you to explore the art within yourself. There you will find the beginning of your own masterpiece.

Margaret Shields Marti

Margaret Shields Marti

Ladybug

Even from a distance, the elements of the ladybug quilt,
easy-to-piece blocks and a background quilted all in red,
add up to a design that satisfies at many levels. Examine it more closely,
and you'll discover the button spots that help identify these
bugs as the friendly kind.

Finished quilt size: 33½" x 33½"

Number of blocks and finished size: Four blocks, each 7" x 7"

Materials

Red: ¼ yard
   Pieces to cut: 32 (template A)

Black: scraps
   Pieces to cut: 16 (template D)

Apricot: 1⅝ yards
   Pieces to cut: 64 (template B), 48 (template C), 32 (template E), 1 (6½" square) for center, 1 (35½" square) for backing

White: 1 yard
   Pieces to cut: 68 (template E), 4 (template F), 4 (template G), 4 (1" x 6½"), 4 yards of 1½"-wide bias strips for binding

Gray: 1 yard
   Pieces to cut: 4 (7" x 35½") for border

Polyester fleece: 1 yard
   Pieces to cut: 1 (33½" square)

Red thread for quilting
Green embroidery floss
48 (³/₈"-wide) black flat buttons

Quilt Top Assembly

Note: All seam allowances are ¼".

1. Piece the ladybug blocks. Join two red As on long edge. Join one apricot B to each corner of the A/A unit to complete one A/B square.

Join a C to right and left edges of A/B square.

Join one apricot E to each end of one black D. Join one white E to each apricot E. Join D/E unit to top edge of A/B/C unit (Diagram 1).

Join one white E to each end of one C. Join E/C unit to bottom edge of A/B/C unit to complete ladybug square. Repeat to make 15 more ladybug squares.

Join four ladybug squares, with the head of each bug facing the right-hand side of the next (see photo). Repeat to make three more ladybug blocks.

Transfer quilting lines (dotted lines) and embroidery lines (solid lines) to the C strips on right and left sides of each ladybug square (Diagram 2). Backstitch with two strands of floss to embroider leg lines.

2. Piece the center block. Join 1" x 6½" white strips to right and left edges of the 6½" apricot square. Join one white E to each end of one remaining 1" x 6½" white strip. Repeat to make another pieced strip. Join strips to top and bottom edges of square, to complete center block.

3. Assemble the quilt center. Join a ladybug block to one edge of the center block. Repeat for opposite edge. Join Fs to opposite ends of this strip (Diagram 3). Join Gs to right and left edges of a third ladybug block. Join an F to top edge. Repeat once to make another ladybug/F/G unit. Join ladybug/F/G units to top and bottom edges of center strip, to complete quilt center.

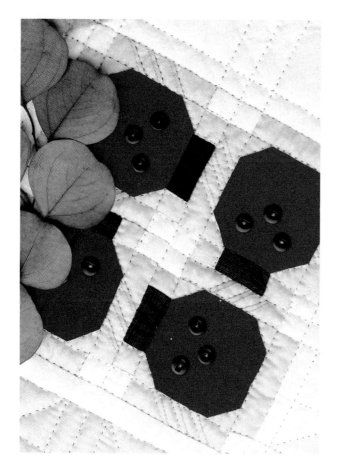

Finishing

1. Bind the edges. Join white bias strips to make a continuous length and use to bind edges of quilt.

2. Add the buttons. Sew three black buttons onto each ladybug (see photo) stitching through all layers.

Layout Schematic

4. Add the border. Center and stitch one gray border strip to each edge of quilt top. Miter the corners (Layout Schematic).

Quilting

1. Mark the quilting design. Mark remaining quilting lines as shown (Quilting Schematic).

2. Stack the layers. Stack the quilt backing (right side down), fleece, and quilt top. Baste securely through all layers.

3. Quilt. Quilt on all marked lines with red thread. Also quilt ⅛″ inside seams on ladybug bodies, in-the-ditch outside ladybug bodies, and along each seam in ladybug blocks.

Trim edges of backing and fleece to match quilt top.

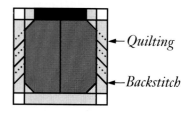

Diagram 1: Completing a Ladybug Square

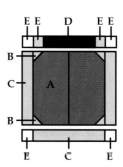

Diagram 2

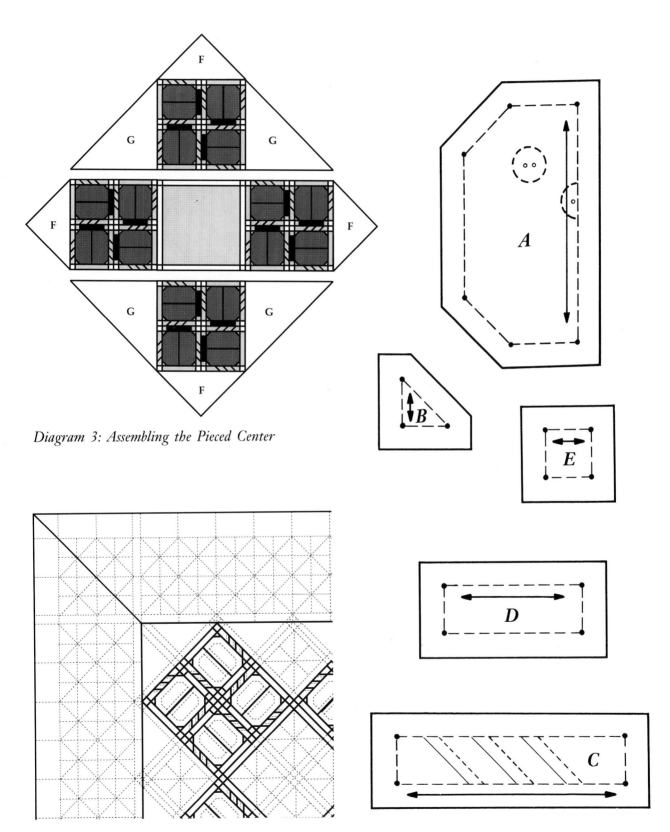

Diagram 3: Assembling the Pieced Center

Quilting Schematic
Note: Dotted lines indicate quilting.

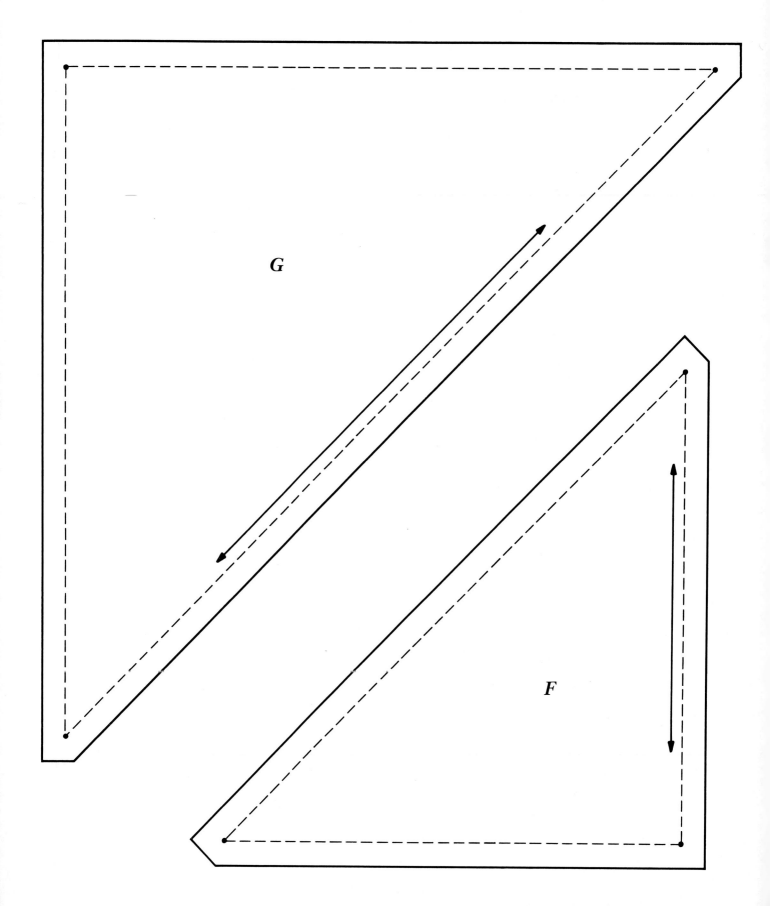

Log Cabin Rose

*Take a second look at our patchwork rose design, and you'll discover that
it's really an old friend, the log cabin block,
dressed up by some extra piecing within the strips. Lines of satin-stitch
embroidery add rich detailing to the center of each rose.*

Finished size of quilt: 26" x 26"

Number of blocks and finished size: nine blocks, each 7" x 7"

Materials

Red polished cotton: ⅛ yard
  Pieces to cut: 1 (1¼" x 11¼"), 1 (1½" x 36")

White: ⅝ yard
  Pieces to cut: 1 (¾" x 11¼"), 1 (¾" x 13½"), 16 (template B), 4 (2¼" x 28") for border

Gray-on-white stripe: ¼ yard
  Pieces to cut: 36 (template A), 58½" total (1¼"-wide strips)

Gray-on-white windowpane: ⅛ yard
  Pieces to cut: 1 (1½" x 13½"), 1 (1¼" x 11¼")

Lt. green: ¼ yard
  Pieces to cut: 1 (1¾" x 15¾"), 4 (⅞" x 28") for border, 18 (template A)

Dk. green: ⅛ yard
  Pieces to cut: 18 (template A)

Gray print: 1¼ yards
  Pieces to cut: 76½" (1¾"-wide) strips, 3 yards of 1¼"-wide bias strips for binding

Pink: ⅜ yard
  Pieces to cut: 20 (template B)

Green print: ⅞ yard
  Pieces to cut: 1 (28" square) for backing

Polyester fleece: ¾ yard
  Pieces to cut: 1 (26" square)

White embroidery floss for satin-stitch embroidery
Gray thread for quilting

Quilt Top Assembly

Note: All seam allowances are ¼".

1. Piece nine red blocks. Place 1¼" x 11¼" red strip and ¾" x 11¼" white strip with right sides together. Join along one long edge. Open up strip and finger-press seam allowance toward red strip. Cutting across the band, cut nine 1¼" segments. (Note: To prevent unraveling, machine-stitch seams when using this technique.) Sew remaining ¾"-wide white strip to left edge of one segment (Diagram 1); trim off unused portion of strip. Add two 1½"-wide red strips to block, using same stitch-and-cut system (Diagram 2). Repeat this process to make eight more blocks.

2. Make triangle strips. Join a striped A to a light green A to make a striped/light green A/A square. Repeat to make 17 more. Join remaining striped As to dark green As to make 18 striped/dark green A/A squares.

Join one light green A/A square to one dark green A/A square to make a triangle strip as shown (Diagram 3). Repeat to make eight more. In a similar manner, make nine triangle strips that are mirror images of the first set (Diagram 3).

3. Add triangle strips to the block. Join a triangle strip from the first set to the lower edge of red block as shown (Diagram 4). Repeat to join remaining strips from first set to remaining red blocks.

Cut the 1½"-wide windowpane fabric strips into nine 1½" squares. Join a windowpane square to end of each remaining triangle strip (the second set), sewing each square to a dark green triangle.

Join one of these strips to left edge of each red block, with green triangles to the outside.

4. Add striped strips. Sew a striped strip to top edge of each square as shown (Diagram 5). Trim off excess fabric. Cut the 1¼"-wide windowpane strip into nine 1¼" squares. Cut remaining 1¼"-wide striped fabric into 3½" long strips. Sew a windowpane square to one

Quilting

1. Mark the quilting design. Mark all quilting lines (Quilting Schematic).

2. Stack the layers. Stack the quilt backing (right side down), fleece, and top. Baste securely through all layers.

Quilt with gray thread on every seam line of pieced center blocks, on both sides of border, and on all marked quilting lines. (Do not quilt on seams that join the pink and white triangles.)

Trim backing and fleece to match quilt top.

Finishing

1. Bind the edges. Join 1¼"-wide gray print strips to make a continuous length of binding and use to bind edges of quilt.

end of each strip. Sew a striped/windowpane strip to right side of each block, with windowpane square at top.

5. Add gray strips. Join 1¾"-wide gray print strip to bottom edge of each square. Trim. Cut remaining gray fabric into 4¼" strips. Cut 1¾" light green strip into 1¾" squares. Add a square to one end of each gray strip. Join a gray/light green strip to left side of each block, with green square at bottom.

6. Complete the blocks. Join four white triangle Bs to sides of one block (Diagram 6). Repeat with three more blocks. Join four pink triangle Bs to sides of one block. Repeat for remaining blocks. Satin-stitch by hand with two strands of white floss to cover entire surface of ¼"-wide white strips that frame the red square at center of each block.

7. Join the blocks. Join blocks together, alternating blocks with pink Bs and white Bs (see photo).

8. Add the border. Join narrow light green strips to white border strips. Join green/white strips to quilt top, with green fabric to the inside. Miter the corners.

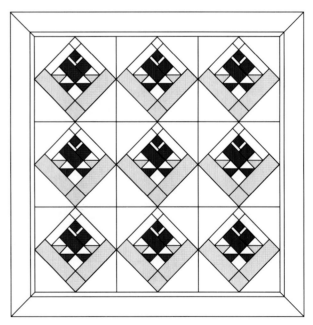

Layout Schematic

Diagram 1

Diagram 2

Diagram 3

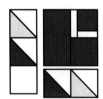

Diagram 4

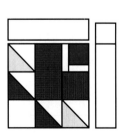

Diagram 5

Diagram 6

Quilting Schematic
Note: Dotted lines indicate quilting.

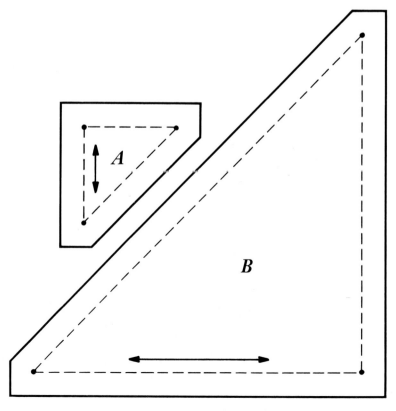

Blue and White Stars

Shaded diagonal rows of squares and sparkling stars suggest a quilt set on point. But the blocks are actually joined in horizontal rows. The movement of the design is created entirely through careful selection and placement of color.

Quilt Top Assembly

Note: All seam allowances are ¼".

1. Piece the 49-square block. Make striped fabric by
joining 33" strips in this order: one blue minicheck,
one print, three white, one print, and one blue minicheck (Diagram 1). Cut across the fabric to divide it
into 22 (1½"-wide) strips of squares. (Note: To prevent
unraveling, machine-stitch when using this technique.)

Join additional 33" strips in this order: one print, one
check, one print, one white, one print, one check, and
one print (Diagram 2, row 2). Cut as before to make 22
more strips of 1½" squares as shown.

Using Diagram 2, row 3, as a guide to colors and
placement, join and cut 24" strips to make 16 strips of
squares.

Join and cut 12" strips as shown (Diagram 2, row 4)
to make eight strips of squares. Lay out rows of squares
in order shown (Diagram 2) and join to complete one
(49-square) block. Repeat to make seven more blocks.

Join the remaining row 1 and row 2 strips in pairs to
make six (14-square) border blocks (Diagram 3).

Join the two remaining 12" check and print strips.
Cut across band at 1½" intervals to make eight check/
print rectangles. Join pairs of rectangles to make four
checkerboard corner squares for border of quilt.

2. Piece the star blocks. Join a blue A to each long
edge of one blue check B (Diagram 4) to make a
right-angle triangle. Repeat to make one more blue/
check A/B triangle and two blue/print A/B triangles.

Join one check and one print triangle to make a large
triangle. Repeat to make one more. Join the two large
triangles as shown to make a star square. Join one
white D to each edge of star square.

Join white Fs to outside edges of D/star square unit
(Diagram 5). Join one blue C to each corner between
Fs to complete star block. Repeat to make six more star
blocks.

3. Piece the border. Join blue Cs to ends of one print
E. Repeat to make nine more C/E border blocks.

4. Piece the top. Lay out the quilt top in rows,
including the border blocks (Layout Schematic). Join
the blocks to make rows as shown; then join the rows
to complete the top.

Join blue checkered border strips to quilt top, placing long strips on right and left edges and short strips
on top and bottom edges.

Quilting

1. Mark the quilting design. Mark all quilting lines
for star blocks and C/E border blocks as shown (Quilting Schematic).

2. Stack the layers. Stack quilt backing, fleece, and
quilt top. Baste securely through all layers.

3. Quilt. Quilt on all marked lines with the white
thread. Quilt as close as possible to seam lines of each
small square in the 49-square blocks. Trim edges of
backing and fleece to match top.

Finishing

1. Bind the edges. Join blue bias strips to make a continuous length and use strip to bind edges of quilt.

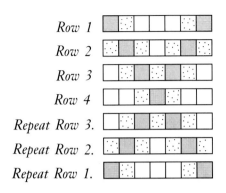

Diagram 2: Assembling 49-Square Block

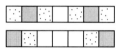

Diagram 3: Assembling 14-Square
Border Block

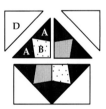

Diagram 4

Layout Schematic

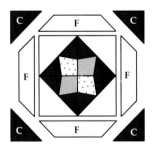

Diagram 5

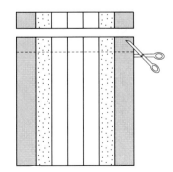

Diagram 1: Piecing Row 1

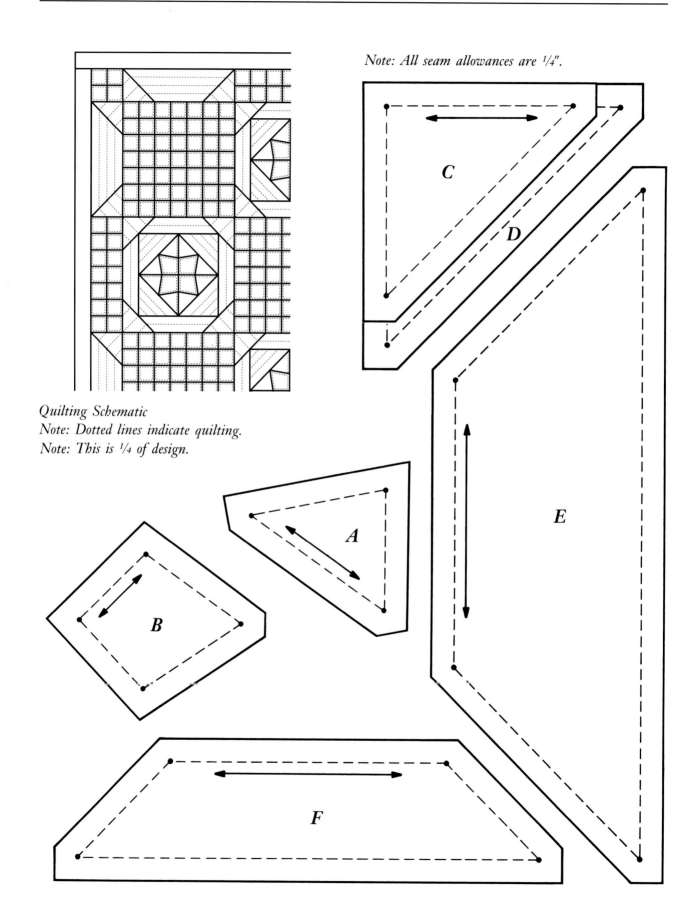

Note: All seam allowances are ¼".

C

D

A

B

E

F

Quilting Schematic
Note: Dotted lines indicate quilting.
Note: This is ¼ of design.

Gardener's Dream

There's never a need to feed or spray these lovely roses, and they are always in full bloom. Although the patchwork design may look involved, the puzzle will come together like magic when you join the strips that make up each block.

Finished size of quilt: 34½" x 34½"

Number of blocks and finished size: five (10" x 10") blocks; four pieced triangles

Materials

Cream/cream print: ¾ yard
Pieces to cut: 9 (template A), 5 (template B), 5 (template C), 40 (template E), 5 (template G), 18 (template H), 10 (template I), 4 (template J), 8 (template S), 8 (template Q)

Peach: ¼ yard
Pieces to cut: 19 (template D), 19 (template F)

Peach print: ⅜ yard
Pieces to cut: 19 (template D), 19 (template F), 4 (template K)

Rose: ⅛ yard
Pieces to cut: 19 (template F)

Green print: ⅜ yard
Pieces to cut: 4 (template U), 4 (template T), 5 (template D), 5 (template E), 10 (template H), 5 (template G), 16 (template L)

Sage green: 1¼ yards
Pieces to cut: 5 (template C), 18 (template E), 4 (template J), 8 (template R), 1 (36½" square) for backing

Dk. green print: 1¼ yards
Pieces to cut: 24 (template M), 16 (template N), 4 (template O), 4 (template P), 2 (1¼" x 32½"), 8 (1¼" x 10") and 2 (1¼" x 12") for sashing, 4 yards of 1½"-wide bias strips for binding

Batting: 1 yard
Pieces to cut: 34½" square

Cream thread for quilting

Quilt Top Assembly

Note: All seam allowances are ¼".

1. Make the five rose squares. Each block contains nine strips or rows. Using Diagram 1 as a guide, make the rows as follows:

Row 1: Use 1 cream A.
Row 2: Join a cream B and a peach D.
Row 3: Join a cream I, a peach D, a cream H, a peach print F, a rose F, a peach F, and a cream H as shown.
Row 4: Join a cream G, a peach print F, a rose F, a peach F, a green print H, a peach print D, and a green print D.
Row 5: Join a cream E, a sage E, a peach print D, a peach D, a sage C, and a cream E.
Row 6: Join a cream E, a green print G, a peach print F, a rose F, a peach F, a green print H, and a cream E.
Row 7: Join a cream E, a sage E, a peach print D, and a cream I.
Row 8: Join a cream E, a green print E, a cream E.
Row 9: Use a cream E.
Join rows 1-9 as shown to make a peach rose block. Repeat to make four more blocks.

2. Piece the rose triangles. Join pieces as shown (Diagram 2) to make rows 1-4.
Row 1: Use one cream A.
Row 2: Join a cream Q, a peach D, and a cream Q.
Row 3: Join a sage R, a cream H, a peach print F, a rose F, a peach F, a cream H, a sage R.
Row 4: Join a cream S, a sage E, a peach print D, a sage E, and a cream S.
Join rows 1-4 as shown to form a triangle. Repeat to make three more triangles.

3. Piece the quilt top. Join 1¼" x 10" dark green print strips to opposite edges of one rose block as shown (Diagram 3). Repeat with three more blocks. Place the remaining rose block between two dark green-edged blocks and join to make a strip. Join two peach print Ks to ends of this strip (Diagram 4) to complete center band of quilt top.

Join a 1¼" x 12" dark green print strip to the long edge of one remaining K. Join the dark green-edged K and two rose triangles to one dark green-edged rose square as shown (Diagram 4) to make a large triangle. Repeat to make a second triangle that is a mirror image of the first.

Place 1¼" x 32½" dark green print strips between the center band and the large triangles. Join to complete quilt top. Trim ends of dark green strips to match edge of quilt.

4. Piece the border. Join one dark green print N to one green print L as shown (Diagram 5). Join a dark green print M to the left edge of the N/L unit. Repeat to make three more M/N/L units.

Join two M/N/L units as shown (Diagram 6), with a dark green print M between, to make left end of border strip. Repeat to make a second mirror-image strip for the right end.

Join a dark green print O to a green print T as shown (Diagram 7). Join a dark green print P to a green print U. Join the O/T unit and the P/U unit to opposite edges of a sage J as shown, to complete center unit of border strip.

To complete border strip, join left and right ends of border to center (Diagram 8). Repeat to make three more border strips.

5. Add the border. Match point of J on one border strip to lower left corner of rose on bottom edge of quilt top (Layout and Quilting Schematic). Join the border strip to the quilt top. Repeat with three additional border strips. Join corners.

Quilting

1. Mark the quilting design. Mark quilting lines in the four peach print triangle Ks. Draw a line from the outside corner of the triangle to the center of the long edge. Mark parallel lines 1" apart as shown (Layout and Quilting Schematic) to fill triangle.

2. Stack the layers. Stack the quilt backing (right side down), batting, and quilt top. Baste securely through all layers.

3. Quilt. Quilt in-the-ditch with cream thread around the center square of each rose, around the outside of each whole rose, and on all remaining seams. Quilt along lines marked in corner Ks. Trim edges of backing and batting to match top.

Finishing

1. Bind the edges. Join the dark green bias strips to make a continuous length and bind edges of quilt.

Layout and Quilting Schematic
Note: Dotted lines indicate quilting.

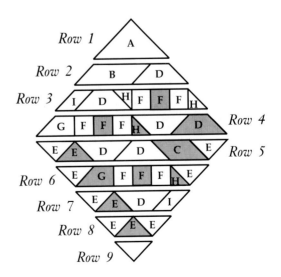

Diagram 1

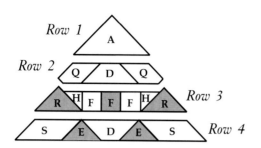

Row 1
A
Row 2
Q
D
Q
R
H
F
F
F
H
R
Row 3
S
E
D
E
S
Row 4

Diagram 2

M
L
N
M

Diagram 6

O
T
J
P
U

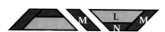

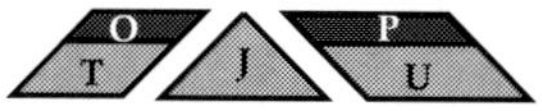

Diagram 7

Diagram 3

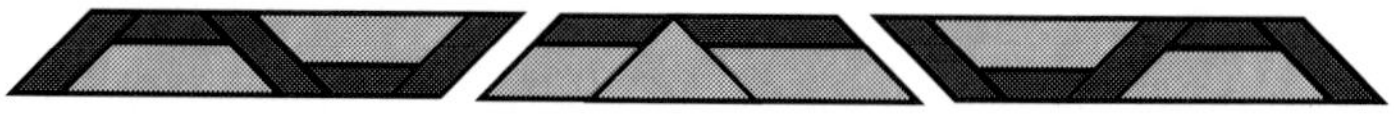

Diagram 8

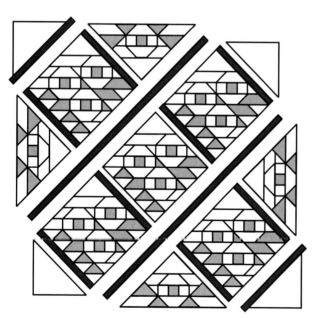

Diagram 4

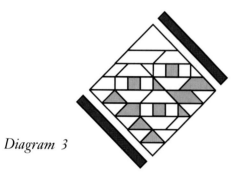

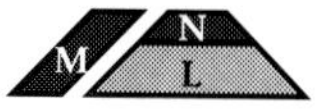

Cut half of pieces with template reversed.
Q
R

M
N
L

Diagram 5

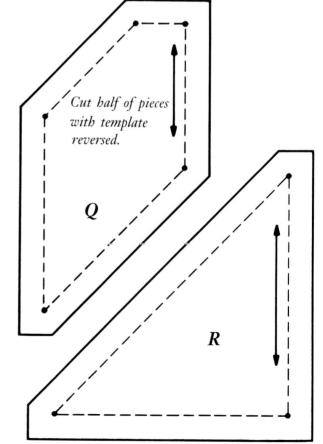

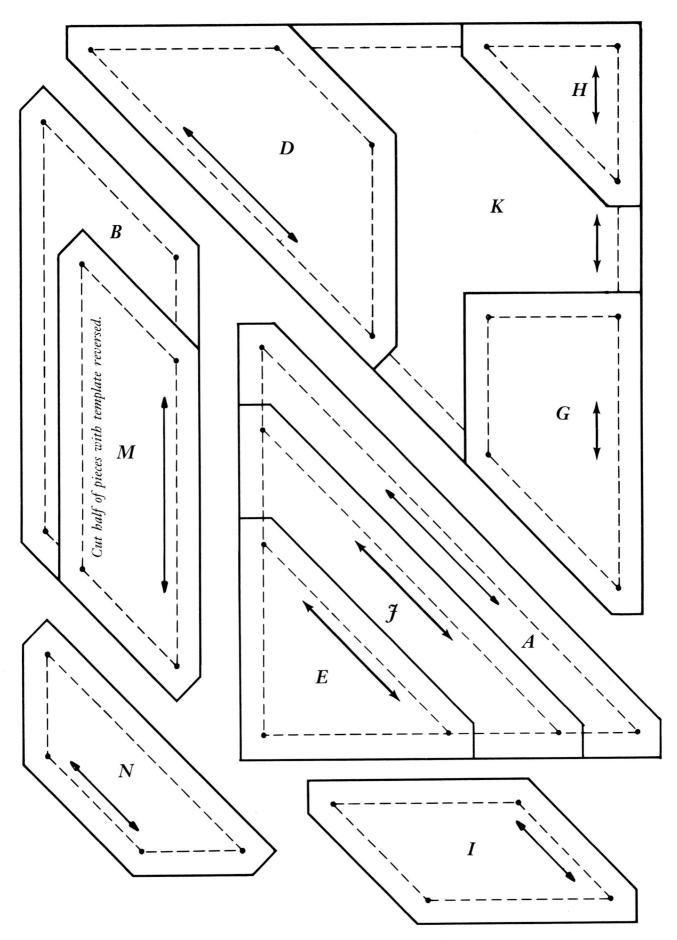

Cut half of pieces with template reversed.

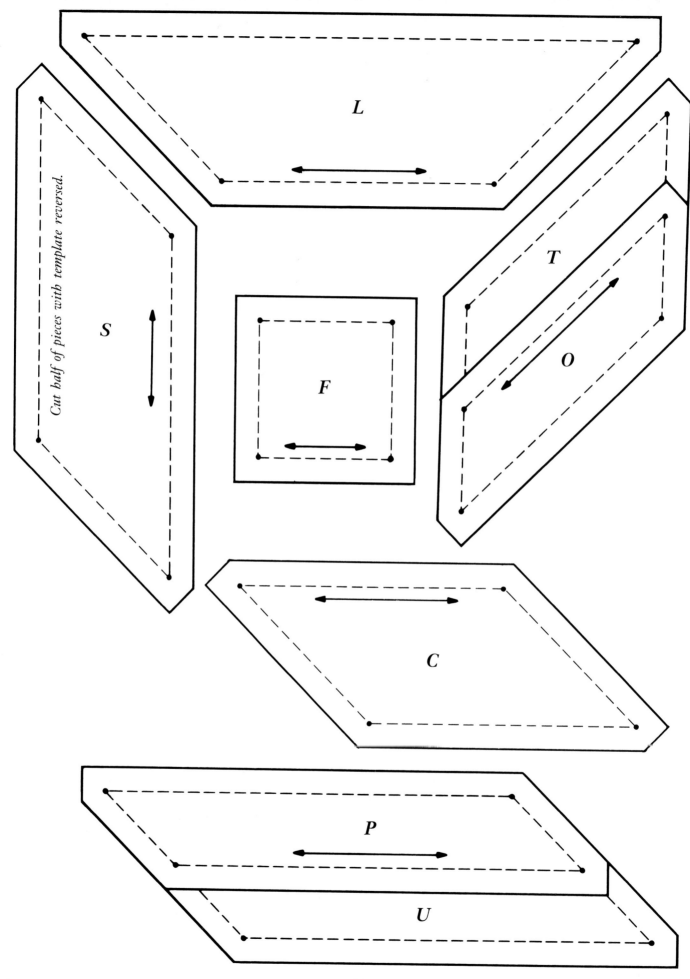

L

Cut half of pieces with template reversed.

S

F

T

O

C

P

U

Tumbling Rainbow

*Cascading shades of color seem to drip from a cloud and ripple
across the lower edge of this dramatic hanging.
Despite its visual intricacy, this is not a hard quilt to make. It has only
one pattern piece and can be assembled at the sewing machine.*

Finished size of quilt: *19½″ x 38¼″*

Materials

White: 1½ yards
Pieces to cut: 1 (21½″ x 40¼″) for backing, 5¾ yards of 2″-wide strips, 11 (template A)

Note: Template A is used to cut all colored pieces.
Shades of green (1-5): scraps
Pieces to cut: 4 (shade 1), 1 each (shades 2, 3, 4, 5)

Shades of teal (1-5): scraps
Pieces to cut: 4 (shade 1), 2 (shade 2), 1 each (shades 3, 4, 5)

Shades of blue (1-5): scraps
Pieces to cut: 5 (shade 1), 2 (shade 2), 2 (shade 3), 1 each (shades 4, 5)

Shades of violet (1-5): scraps
Pieces to cut: 5 (shade 1), 2 each (shades 2, 3, 4), 1 (shade 5)

Shades of purple (1-5): scraps
Pieces to cut: 5 (shade 1), 2 each (shades 2, 3, 4, 5)

Shades of rose (1-5): scraps
Pieces to cut: 4 (shade 1), 2 each (shades 2, 3, 4, 5)

Shades of orange (1-5): scraps
Pieces to cut: 3 (shade 1), 1 each (shades 2, 3, 4, 5)

Flannel: 5/8 yard
Pieces to cut: 1 (19½″ x 38¼″)

White thread for quilting background
Embroidery floss to match middle shade in each of the seven color families for quilting

Quilt Top Assembly

Note: All seam allowances are ¼″.

1. Piece the vertical rows. Using Layout Schematic as a guide, cut 2″-wide strips of white into segments as follows:

Row 1: 7¼″
Row 2: 11¾″
Row 3: 5″
Row 4: 11¾″
Row 5: 9½″ and 7¼″
Row 6: 16¼″
Row 7: 14″
Row 8: 20¾″
Row 9: 18½″
Row 10: 7¼″ and 16¼″
Row 11: 23″ and 7¼″
Row 12: 14″ and 14″
Row 13: 27½″ and 7¼″

Piece each vertical row from top to bottom, referring to Layout Schematic for placement of colors. Begin with the lightest shade of each color (1) at the top of the quilt and graduate to the darkest shade (5) at the bottom. Insert the white strips, white As, and additional colored blocks as shown (Layout Schematic). Join the rows to complete the quilt top.

Quilting and Finishing

1. Mark the quilting design. On all white areas, mark horizontal lines ¼″ apart. On all colored areas, mark vertical lines ¼″ apart.

2. Stack the layers. Stack the backing (right side down), flannel, and quilt top, aligning top and right-hand edges. Baste through all layers. Trim backing and flannel to match lower left stair-step edge of the quilt. Then trim ¼″ seam allowance from all edges of flannel. Fold seam allowances of backing and top to inside and slipstitch together to join. (It may be necessary to remove a few stitches from seams along stair-step edges, in order to fold under seam allowance.)

Layout Schematic

Note: All colored pieces cut from template A are numbered 1-5. (Highest number within each color indicates darkest color.) White pieces cut from template are labeled A.

Row – 1	2	3	4	5	6	7	8	9	10	11	12	13
G1							A					
							R1					
		B1										
		A							V1			
G1		B1		P1								
G2	T1	A	V1									
G3	T2	B1	A			O1					T1	
G4	T3	B2	V1		R1	A						
G5	T4	B3	V2	P1	A	O1		P1				
	T5	B4	V3	P2	R1	A		A				
		B5	V4	P3	R2	O1		P1		B1		
			V5	P4	R3	O2	R1	A	V1			
				P5	R4	O3	R2	P1	A			G1
					R5	O4	R3	P2	V1		T1	
						O5	R4	P3	V2	B1	A	
							R5	P4	V3	B2	T1	
								P5	V4	B3	T2	G1

Note: All seam allowances are ¹/₄".

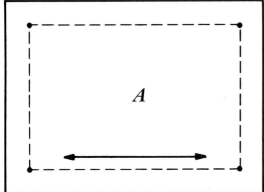

27

Irish Christmas

*Stylized shamrocks lend a touch of the Emerald Isle to this holiday quilt.
The subtle tones of the fabrics make it
equally suitable for use year-round.*

Finished size of quilt: *36" x 36"*

Materials

Dk. rose print: ¹/₂ yard
 Pieces to cut: 4 (1³/₄" x 12¹/₂"), 4 (5" x 31¹/₂") for border

Pink polished cotton: ¹/₄ yard
 Pieces to cut: 4 (template A)

Mauve polished cotton: ³/₈ yard
 Pieces to cut: 2 (9³/₈" square), 2 (template C)

Green: ¹/₄ yard
 Pieces to cut: 20 (template D), 12 (template F)

Green/white print: ¹/₈ yard
 Pieces to cut: 20 (template D)

Green/white stripe: ¹/₈ yard
 Pieces to cut: 16 (template D)

Green/white pindot: ¹/₈ yard

Pieces to cut: 20 (template D)

Green/dk. green print: ¹/₄ yard
 Pieces to cut: 16 (template D), 12 (template I)

Pink/white pindot: ¹/₈ yard
 Pieces to cut: 4 (template G), 4 (template H), 12 (template J)

Rose/burgundy print: 1¹/₂ yards
 Pieces to cut: 4 (5" square) pieces E, 4 (5" x 18") for border**, 1 (38" square) for backing

Dk. green print: 1¹/₄ yards
 Pieces to cut: 4 (³/₄" x 18"), 4¹/₂ yards of 2"-wide bias strips for binding

Batting: 1 yard
 Pieces to cut: 1 (36" square)

Burgundy, pink, and lt. green thread for quilting

**Note: To be used wrong side up.

Quilt Top Assembly

Note: All seam allowances are ¼″.

1. Piece the center. Join one 12½″ dark rose print strip to the long edge of one pink A. Repeat to make three more dark rose/pink triangles. Join two dark rose/pink triangles on short edges (Diagram 1). Repeat with remaining triangles. Join the two A/A triangles to make a square.

Cut the two 9⅜″ mauve squares on the diagonal to make four B triangles. Join long edge of one B to one edge of square (Diagram 2). Repeat with three remaining triangles to make the center block.

Join long edges of the two mauve Cs together to make a square and fold under ¼″ seam allowance. Center small mauve C/C square in the pink square (Diagram 3) as shown. Trace around small mauve square to mark placement and remove.

Join one green/white print D, one green D, and one green/pindot D to make a 3-petal shamrock. Repeat to make three more.

Place shamrocks on traced square, matching seam lines of shamrocks to placement lines of square (Diagram 3). Appliqué curved edges of shamrocks to pink square. Replace the small mauve square on the pink square, matching edges of mauve square to marked placement line and covering raw edges of shamrocks. Appliqué.

Center and join an 18″ dark green print strip to one edge of the center block. Repeat to join dark green strips to the remaining edges. Miter the corners.

2. Add the borders. Join wrong side of rose/burgundy strips to right side of the center section, on right and left edges. (Wrong side is lighter and will appear to be a different fabric. See photograph.)

Join wrong side of another rose/burgundy strip to right side of a 5″ rose/burgundy E square. Join another square to other end of strip in same way. Repeat to make a second strip/E unit. Join the strip/E units to top and bottom edges of center section.

Join 5″ x 31½″ dark rose print border strips to the left and right edges of the center section. Join remaining strips to top and bottom edges. Lap and join ends of border strips at corners as shown (Layout and Quilting Schematic).

3. Appliqué the border. Join five (one of each color) Ds to make one shamrock. Using the same sequence of colors and prints, make fifteen more shamrocks.

To space shamrocks in rose/burgundy border, mark each border strip off into quarters, making four squares. Trim seam allowance from template D and use it to mark positions for shamrocks on border. Center a shamrock in each square and trace outline. Remove shamrocks.

Appliqué green Fs first. Place one F as shown (Diagram 4), linking outlines of two shamrocks. Turn under seam allowances on F and appliqué. Repeat to join eleven remaining Fs to border.

Appliqué corner pieces next. Pin one pink pindot G to a corner square, linking outlines of shamrocks from two adjacent border strips (Diagram 5). Place pink pindot H as shown, noting that the Gs and Hs intersect in three places on corner squares. (Arrange the pieces so that the H passes under the G at the center.) Appliqué the G and H pieces to the corner, leaving the left 2″ of the H unattached.

Appliqué shamrocks in positions marked on border. Appliqué a green/dark green print I between two shamrocks as shown, placing it ¼″ above and parallel to the green F. When you come to the right end of the I, carefully snip a few stitches to open the seam between the two appropriate shamrock petals (Diagram 5); insert end of I as shown and sew opening closed. Repeat to join remaining Is.

On other side of same petal, snip seam. Insert left end of H and slipstitch closed. Repeat for other Hs. Appliqué pink Js in corners (Layout and Quilting Schematic).

Quilting

1. Mark the quilting design. Mark quilting lines in center square, tracing the Ellipse Quilting Pattern end to end to make the chain design in the inner border strips. Mark lines ¼″ apart to use for echo-quilting around design in appliquéd border, making two or more parallel rows as space allows. Mark a guideline down center of each rose/burgundy print border strip. Center Twisted Cable Quilting Pattern on guidelines at each corner and trace As. Trace Bs along guidelines to fill border as shown (Layout and Quilting Schematic), ending with Cs.

2. Stack the layers. Stack the quilt backing (right side down), batting, and quilt top. Baste securely through all layers, beginning at center and working out.

3. Quilt. Quilt mauve and pink pieces in center with burgundy thread. Quilt in-the-ditch along all seams of shamrocks with light green thread. Quilt Twisted Cable Pattern in outer border with pink thread. Use pink thread to outline-quilt around appliqué in shamrock borders; then echo-quilt to fill remaining space. Trim backing and batting to match top.

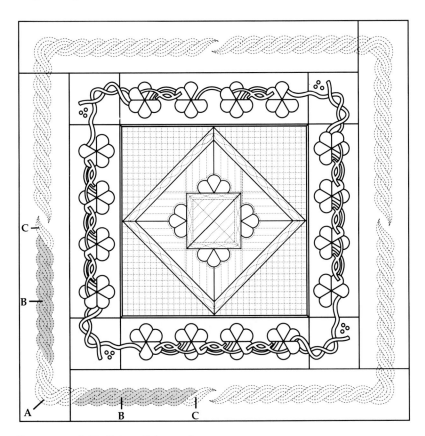

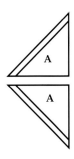

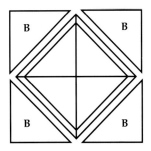

Diagram 1 *Diagram 2*

Finishing

1. Bind the edges. Join the dark green print bias strips to make a continuous length and use strip to bind edges of quilt.

Placement line for C/C square

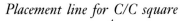

Diagram 3

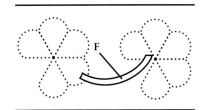

Diagram 4: Positioning Stems

Layout and Quilting Schematic
Note: Dotted lines indicate quilting.

Ellipse Quilting Pattern for Inner Border

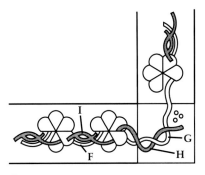

Diagram 5

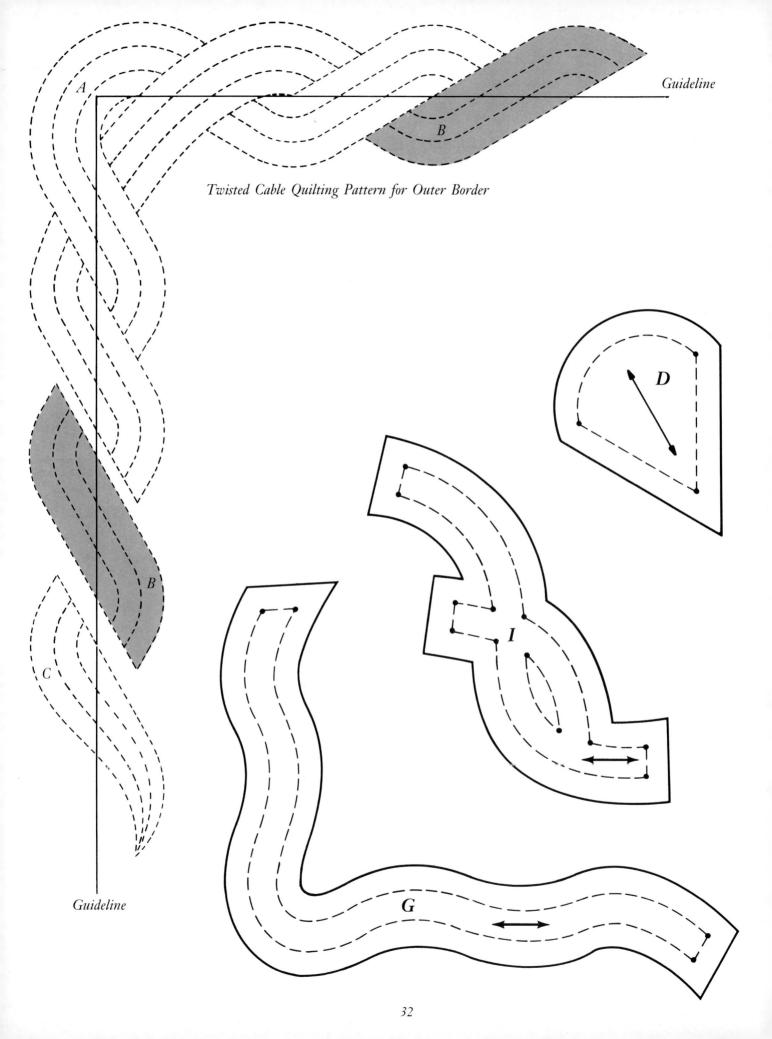

Twisted Cable Quilting Pattern for Outer Border

A

Guideline

B

B

C

D

I

G

Guideline

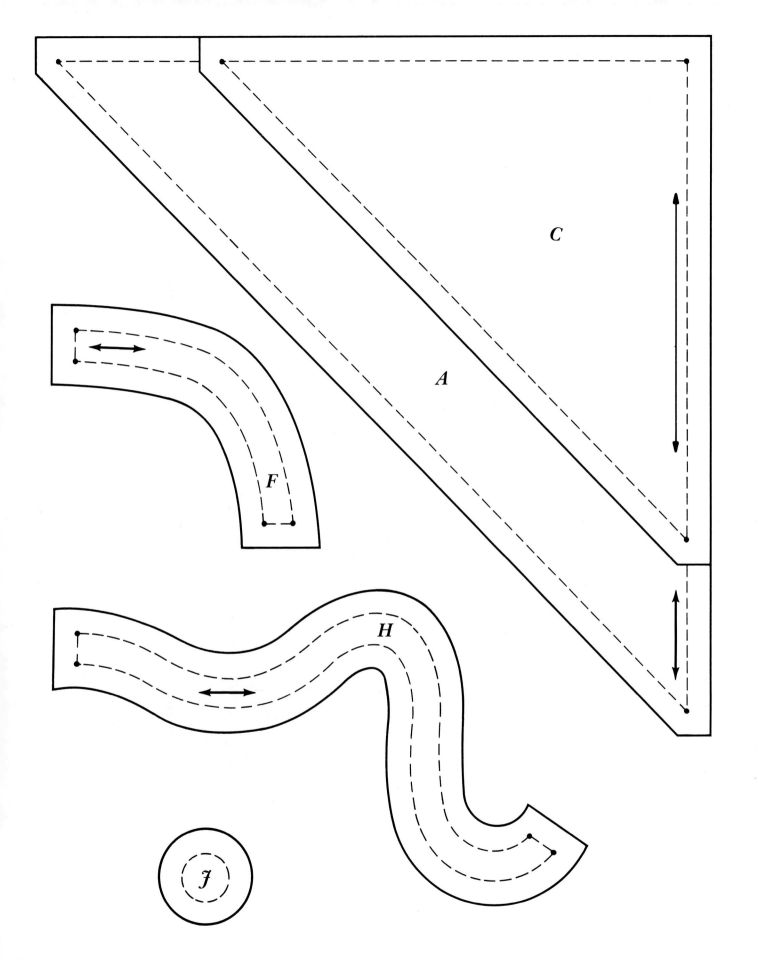

Pastel Tulips

*Half the fun of this doll-sized quilt lies in picking out a bouquet of soft,
springlike colors from which to make it.
Mostly pieced, the quilt sports just one blossom that is appliquéd.
See if you can find it.*

Finished size of quilt: *18" x 23½"*

Number of blocks and finished size: *23 tulip blocks,
2½" x 2½"; six leaf blocks, 2½" x 5"*

Materials

Cream: ¾ yard
Pieces to cut: 1 (20" x 25½") for backing, 30 (template D), 12 (template C)

Cream/pink pindot: ⅜ yard
*Pieces to cut: 1 (2" x 24") for border, 2 (2" x 15") for
border, 1 (3" x 8") piece J, 1 (3" x 5") piece H, 1 (3" x
3") piece I, 3 (template B), 1 (template E), 1 (template E*), 28 (template D), 2 (2" x 3") piece G, 2
(1½" x 3")*

11 assorted cream, pink, and blue prints: scraps
Pieces to cut: 23 (template A), 1 (template F)

Green print: 1 yard
*Pieces to cut: 1 (2" x 24") for border, 6 (template C),
6 (template C*), 12 (template D), 2½ yards of
1"-wide bias strips for binding*

Green: ¼ yard
*Pieces to cut: 12 (template B), 6 (1" x 5½"), 5 (1" x 8"),
1 (1" x 3½")*

Polyester fleece: ⅝ yard
Pieces to cut: 1 (18" x 23½")

Cream, green thread for quilting
Pink embroidery floss
24" (⅛"-wide) pink satin ribbon
18" (⅛"-wide) cream satin ribbon
10" (⅛"-wide) blue satin ribbon

*Note: *Flip or reverse template if fabric is
one-sided.*

Quilt Top Assembly
Note: All seam allowances are ¼".

1. Piece the small tulip blocks. Join two cream Ds to
one print A. Repeat to make eight more A/D units. Set
aside. Join two pindot Ds to one print A. Repeat to
make nine more tulip/pindot units. Set aside. For two
additional A/D pieces, join a pindot D to the left side
of A and a cream D to the right side. On the two

remaining As, join a cream D to the left side and a
pindot D to the right side.

2. Make rows 1 and 2. Join one 2" x 3" piece (G), one
tulip/pindot unit, and one pindot B as shown, to make
a strip (Diagram 1). Join a 3" x 5" piece (H) to top edge
of this strip. Set aside.

Join 2 Es to lower edge of F, leaving opening
between Es. Clip and fold under seam allowance on

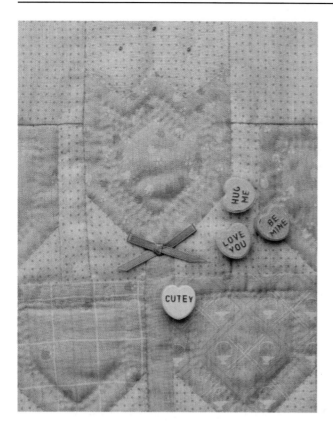

top edge of tulip (F). Appliqué top edge to 3″ x 3″ piece (I), adjusting position so that finished block measures 3″ x 5½″. Set aside.

Join one B, one tulip/pindot block, one B, one tulip/pindot block, and one 2″ x 3″ (G) as shown to make a strip. Join one 3″ x 8″ (J) piece to top edge of this strip.

Join the 3 assembled sections to make one large strip. (Rows 1 and 2 completed.)

3. Make row 3. Join two tulip/pindot blocks, with a green B between. Set aside. Join three more tulip/pindot blocks with green Bs between. Join the two sections to row 2, leaving space between sections as shown (Diagram 2). Fold under top and side seam allowances on 1″ x 3½″ green piece and press. Position this for stem under tulip so that it fills the open space. Slipstitch in place.

4. Make row 4. Join four tulip blocks (two in the center with cream Ds and one on each end with pindot Ds on the outside) with five green Bs between. Join 1½″ x 3″ pindot pieces to ends of row (Layout Schematic).

5. Make row 5. Join five tulip blocks (three in the center with cream Ds and one on each end with pindot

Ds on the outside) with four green Bs between. Join rows 3, 4, and 5 to complete top section.

6. Add the border. Join 2″ x 15″ pindot border strips to left and right-hand edges of top section, aligning bottom edges. Center and join 2″ x 24″ piece to the top edge of section. Miter corners of border.

7. Complete the bottom section. To make leaf units for left side of stems, join one pindot D to one green print C. Join one green print D to one cream C (Diagram 3). Join the two C/D units as shown. Make five more left leaf units, substituting a cream D for the pindot D in each.

Join C*s and remaining Ds as shown to make leaf units for right side of stems (Diagram 4). Make six leaf blocks by joining left and right leaf units, with green 1″ x 5½″ stem pieces between (Diagram 4).

Join a tulip block to top of each leaf block, matching tulips with pindot to leaf blocks with pindot. Join six tulip/leaf blocks with five green 1″ x 8″ stem pieces between, placing pindot tulip blocks on outside edges.

Join green print 2″ x 24″ piece to lower edge of bottom section. Join top and bottom sections together, matching stems on bottom section to tulips on top section as shown.

Quilting

1. Mark the quilting design. Mark lines for echo-quilting ¼″ and ⅜″ inside each tulip piece A, and echo-quilt ¼″, ⅜″, and ½″ inside tulip piece F. Mark diagonal lines ½″ apart on green print part of all leaf blocks. Trace leaf quilting pattern onto border.

2. Stack the layers. Stack the backing (right side down), fleece, and top. Baste securely through all layers.

3. Quilt. Quilt on marked lines of tulips and top border with the cream thread. Quilt in-the-ditch next to the top border with cream. Use green thread to quilt in-the-ditch of all stems and leaves. Quilt the bottom border with green thread.

Finishing

1. Bind the edges. Join green print bias strips to make a continuous length and use to bind edges of quilt.

2. Add embroidery. Embroider three French knots with floss, ¾″ above tulip piece F (Layout Schematic).

3. Add ribbons. Tie three pink, two cream, and one blue 1¼″-wide bows from satin ribbon. Trim ends. Tack to quilt (see photo).

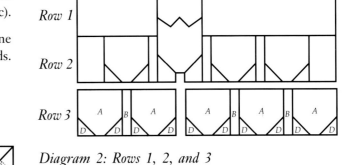

Diagram 2: Rows 1, 2, and 3

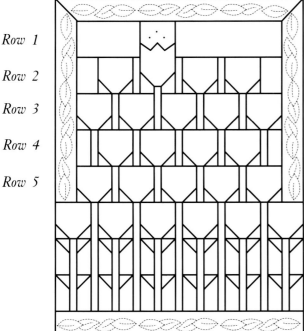

Row 1

Row 2

Row 3

Row 4

Row 5

Layout and Quilting Schematic
Note: Dotted lines indicate quilting.

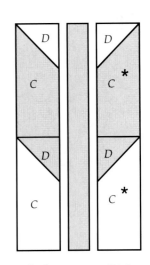

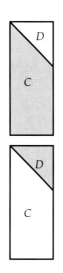

Diagram 3:
Left-hand Leaf Unit

Left   Right
Diagram 4: Assembling
Leaf Block

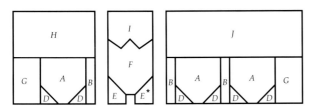

Diagram 1: Rows 1 and 2

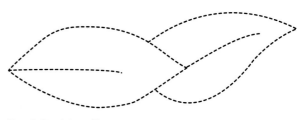

Leaf Quilting Pattern

Note: All seam allowances are ¹⁄₄".

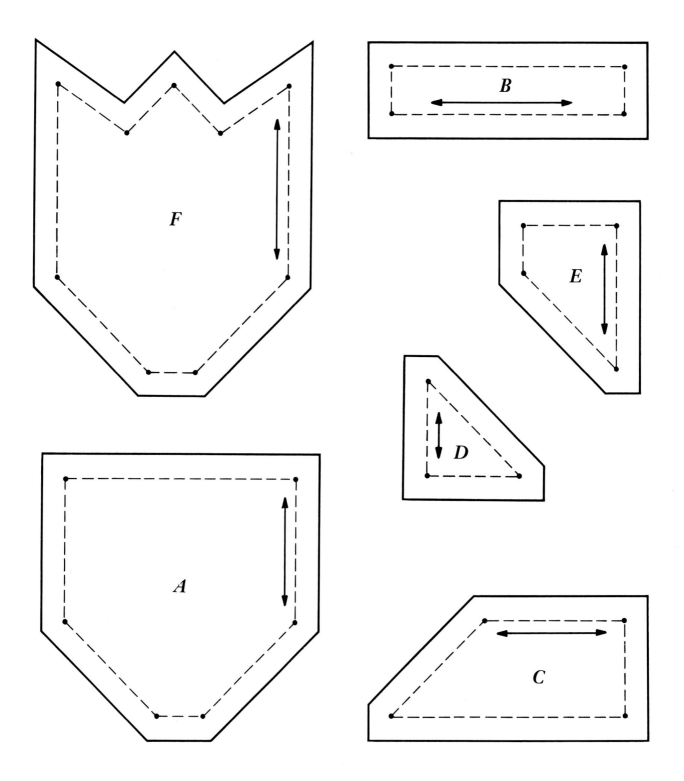

Starburst

Two classic quilt blocks, alternating in checkerboard fashion, create a soothing rhythm in this lap-sized throw. Star blocks and nine-patch blocks interact to create a design as clean and crisp as stars twinkling in the midnight sky.

Quilt Top Assembly

Note: All seam allowances are 1/4".

1. Make the nine-patch blocks. Join navy print As to opposite ends of one white B (Diagram 1). Repeat to make another A/B unit. Join white Bs to opposite edges of one navy print C.

Join A/B units to top and bottom edges of the B/C unit. Repeat to make 12 more nine-patch blocks.

2. Make the star blocks. Join one white D to one gingham D along long edges. Repeat to make seven more D/D units. Join two D/D units as shown (Diagram 2) with white Ds meeting at center. Repeat to make three more D/D strips. Join white As to opposite ends of one D/D strip. Repeat to make another D/A strip.

Join remaining D/D strips to opposite edges of a

gingham C (Diagram 3). Join D/A strips to opposite edges of the D/C strip to complete a star block (Diagram 4). Repeat to make 11 more star blocks.

3. Complete the quilt top. To make row 1, join three nine-patch blocks and two star blocks as shown (Diagram 5), alternating patterns. Repeat to make rows 3 and 5 (Layout Schematic).

Join three star blocks and two nine-patch blocks, alternating patterns to make rows 2 and 4 (Diagram 6). Join the rows as shown (Layout Schematic) to complete pieced top.

4. Add the border. Join 1 1/4" x 30 1/2" white strips to right and left edges of pieced top. Join 1 1/4" x 32" white strips to top and bottom edges. Miter corners.

Join 4 1/2" x 32" navy print strips to right and left edges of the quilt top. Join remaining navy print strips to top and bottom edges (Layout Schematic).

Quilting

1. Mark the quilting design. Mark the floral quilting pattern in the center of each C. Mark three parallel lines 3/8" apart on the white border, centering the middle line.

On the navy print border, mark a quilting line 1/4" in from the seam line, around the outside edge of the quilt (Quilting Schematic). Locate the center of this quilting line on top edge of quilt and mark it with a small dot. Make additional marks along the line at 3/4" intervals, from center to both corners of the quilt.

Repeat process for remaining three edges of quilt.

Using the marks as a guide, draw a grid of diagonal quilting lines to cover the navy print border as shown.

In the same manner, draw a series of lines 3/8" apart along the seam lines and mark a diagonal grid to fill in the white rectangles, triangles, and squares in the quilt center.

2. Stack the layers. Stack the quilt backing (right side down), fleece, and quilt top. Baste securely through all layers.

3. Quilt. Quilt on all marked lines with white thread. Also outline-quilt 1/4" inside seam line on all points of stars and small squares of nine-patch.

Trim the edges of the backing and fleece to match the quilt top.

Finishing

1. Bind the edges. Join the gingham strips to make a continuous length and use to bind the edges.

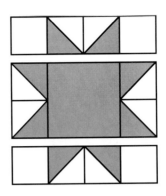

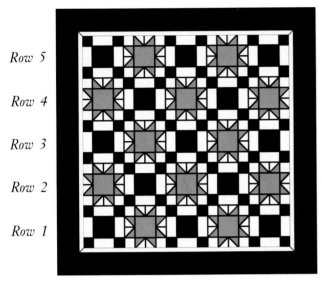

Row 5

Row 4

Row 3

Row 2

Row 1

Layout Schematic

Diagram 4

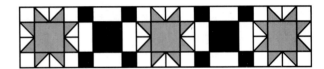

Diagram 5

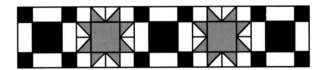

Diagram 6

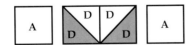

Diagram 1

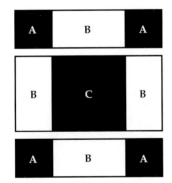

Diagram 2

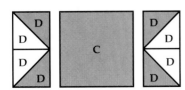

Diagram 3

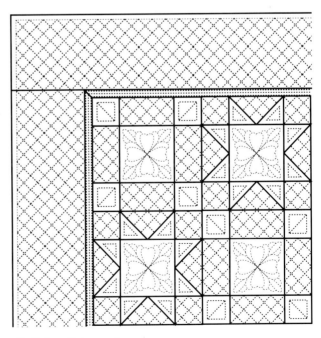

Quilting Schematic
Note: Dotted lines indicate quilting.

Floral Quilting Pattern

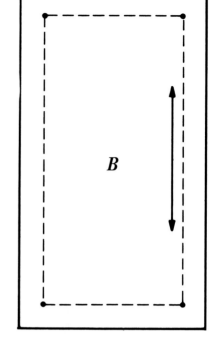

B

Note: All seam allowances are ¼".

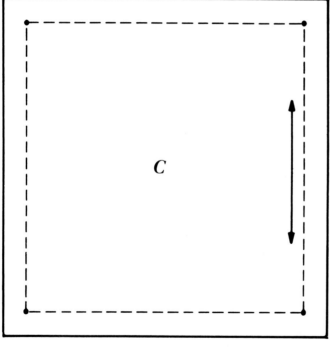

C

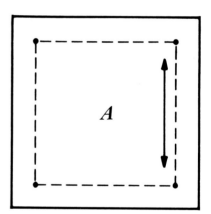

A

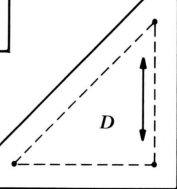

D

Hopscotch and Butterscotch

Large pieces, geometric shapes, and quick-piecing techniques add up to a
wall hanging you can assemble in a hop, skip, and a jump.
The game-boardlike design works especially well in rooms
with a country flavor.

Quilt Top Assembly

Note: All seam allowances are ¼".

1. Piece the five sawtooth blocks. Join four gold/ dark print As and three white As as shown (Diagram 1). Repeat to make nineteen more sawtooth strips.

Join one sawtooth strip to each edge of one gold/ white print 10½" square. Add one white B to each of the four corners as shown (Diagram 2). Repeat to complete four more sawtooth blocks.

2. Piece the four red-square blocks. Join one red pindot 1¾" x 28" strip and one white 1¾" x 28" strip along long edges to make a band of striped fabric. Cut across the band to make 1¾"-wide segments (Diagram 3). Repeat with another pair of red and white strips to make a total of 32 red/white segments. Set aside. (Note: To prevent unraveling, seams should be stitched by machine when using this technique.)

Join the two remaining red pindot strips to long edges of the 3" x 28" white strip. Cut across the band to make 16 (1¾"-wide) strips (Diagram 4).

Join a gold/dark print C, a red/white segment, a gold/white print D, a red/white segment, and a gold/ dark print C as shown (Diagram 5) to make Row 1 of block. Repeat to make row 5.

Join a red/white segment, a gold/white print E, a red/white/red strip, a gold/white print E, and a red/ white segment as shown to make row 2. Repeat to make row 4.

Join a gold/white print D, a red/white/red strip, a gold/white print 5½" square, a red/white/red strip, and a gold/white print D as shown to make row 3.

Join rows 1-5 as shown to complete block. Repeat to make three more red-square blocks.

3. Complete the top. Join the blocks to make three rows of three blocks each as shown (Layout Schematic). Join the rows to complete the top.

Quilting

1. Mark the quilting design. Mark quilting lines on quilt top as shown (Quilting Schematic).

2. Stack the layers. Stack the quilt backing (right side down), batting, and quilt top. Baste securely through all layers.

3. Quilt. Quilt on all marked lines with red thread. Quilt in-the-ditch of all seams with white thread. Trim edges of backing and batting to match quilt top.

Finishing

1. Bind the edges. Join the 2½"-wide white bias strips to make a continuous length. Fold the strip in half, wrong sides together, to make it 1¼" wide. Use folded bias strip to bind edges of quilt.

Layout Schematic

Diagram 1

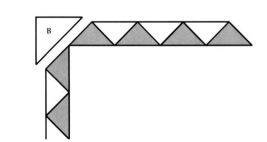

Diagram 2

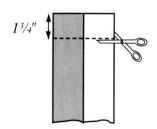

Diagram 3

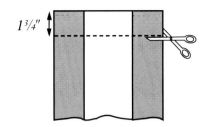

Diagram 4

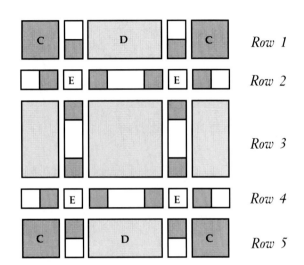

Diagram 5

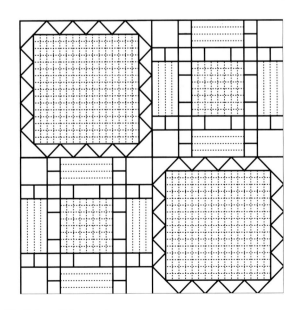

Quilting Schematic
Note: Dotted lines indicate quilting.

45

Note: All seam allowances are ¼".

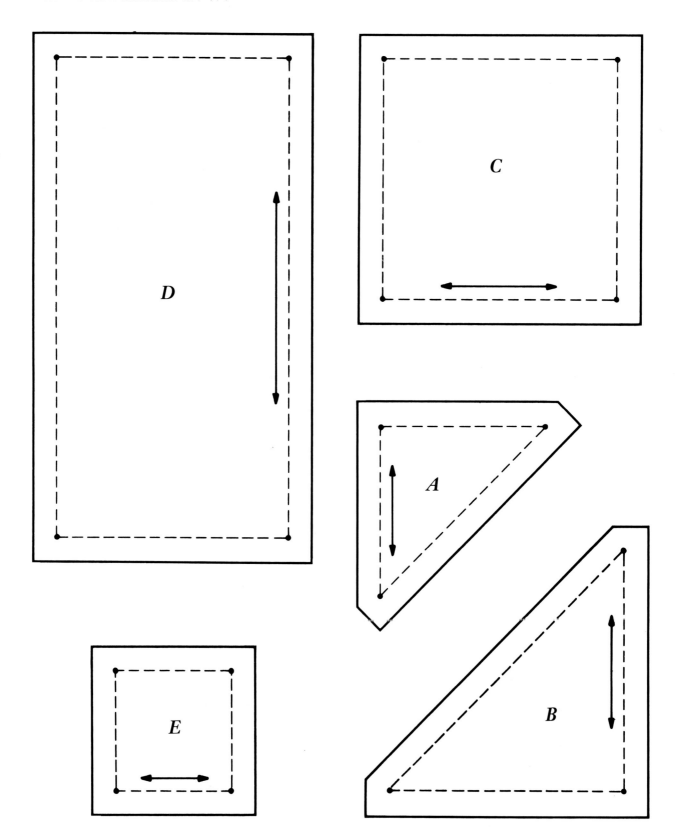

Crazy Hearts

Contrasting values of blue and white make the blocks on this hanging seem like windows, each framing a crazy-quilt landscape. Appliquéd diamonds floating between the hearts create a calming effect, quite different from the high-energy clutter of a typical crazy quilt.

Quilt Top Assembly

Note: All seam allowances are ¼".

1. Construct the hearts. Use template B to trace outline of heart onto center of one 5" muslin square. Cover heart with a variety of blue gray print pieces, arranging shapes in a random manner (Diagram 1). Make sure that fabric edges overlap at least ¼" and fabric extends at least ¼" beyond heart outline. Be sure to include some scraps of the border fabric in your patchwork design.

When you are satisfied with the arrangement, turn under ¼" seam allowance on all exposed edges within heart outline and baste edges to the muslin. Slipstitch folded edges to the muslin. Remove basting.

Position heart pattern over piecing, adjusting location to make best use of fabrics. Mark outline and cut out heart piece, adding ¼" seam allowance as you cut. Repeat to make eleven more hearts.

2. Appliqué and embroider the hearts. Turn under the seam allowance on the hearts. Center each heart on a pindot square (six on right side of pindot fabric and six on wrong side) and appliqué. Buttonhole-stitch around each heart, using two strands of embroidery floss (Diagram 2). Embroider lines of decorative stitching over the seam lines of the appliqués. Here and there, embroider additional areas within selected fabric pieces, using the pattern in the print as a guide. (For example, cover a row of pindots with cross-stitches or embellish calico flowers with lazy-daisy stitch petals and leaves.)

3. Piece the quilt top. To make row 1, join three heart blocks side by side in the following manner: at left, a block with pindots right-side up; at center, a block with pindots wrong-side up; at right, a block with pindots right-side up.

Join 3 blocks for row 2 as follows: at left, pindots wrong-side up; at center, pindots right-side up; at right, pindots wrong-side up.

Continue to join blocks in checkerboard fashion (alternating right and wrong side of pindot blocks) to complete rows 3 and 4.

Join rows 1-4 to complete piecing of quilt center.

4. Add the border. Center and join 2" x 28" blue/gray print strips to top and bottom edges of quilt. Center and join 2" x 35½" strips to side edges. Miter strips at the corners.

5. Add the tan appliqués. Turn under seam allowances on all tan As and baste. Place squares on point at corners of blocks, centering each square over junction of pindot blocks (Layout Schematic). Match corners of tan squares to seam lines of pindot blocks as shown. Appliqué tan squares to quilt top.

Quilting

1. Mark the quilting design. Mark the quilting lines

for blocks and diamonds as shown on Layout Schematic. Mark quilting patterns in blue border of quilt as follows: One corner motif in each corner and two border motifs between each pair of diamonds.

2. Stack the layers. Stack the quilt backing (right side down), fleece, and quilt top. Baste securely through all layers. Trim edges to match quilt top.

3. Quilt. With white thread, quilt in-the-ditch around each block, heart, and diamond, and on all marked lines.

Finishing

1. Bind the edges. Join tan bias fabric strips to make a continuous length and use to bind edges of quilt.

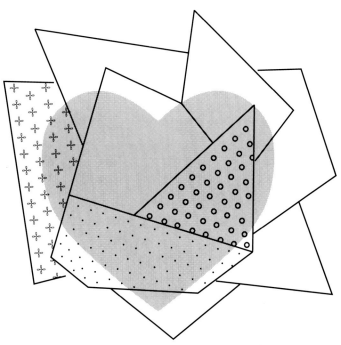

Diagram 1
Note: Shaded area indicates position of heart outline under fabric pieces.

Layout Schematic
Note: Dotted lines indicate quilting.

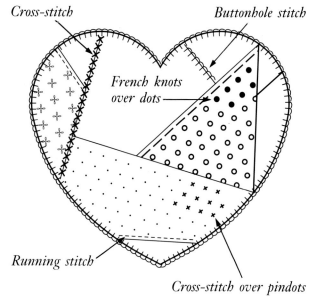

Diagram 2

Note: A ¼" seam allowance is included on template A. Template B has no seam allowance; add ¼" seam allowance when cutting out the fabric.

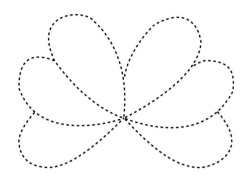

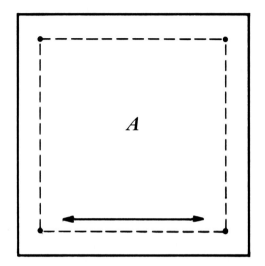

Quilting Pattern for Corner

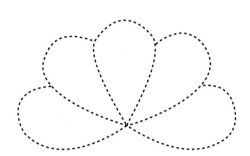

Quilting Pattern for Border

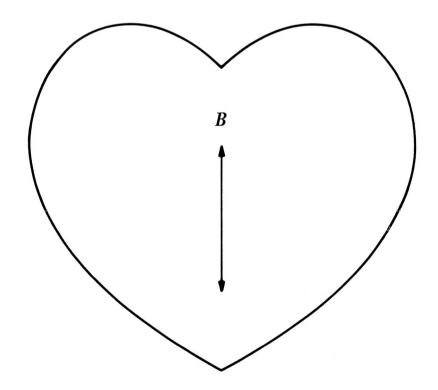

Gray and Green Geometry

Sometimes a bit of appliqué can turn a patchwork puzzle into pure pleasure. Here, crisscrossing strips of gray bias tape make the central star design seem more complex, while actually simplifying the stitching. Appliquéd blocks that repeat the burgundy points of the star enrich the border as well.

Quilt Top Assembly

Note: All seam allowances are ¼".

1. Piece the center block. Join burgundy Cs to opposite ends of a blue-green B. Repeat to make another C/B unit. Join blue-green Bs to opposite edges of a burgundy A. Join C/B units to opposite edges of B/A unit as shown (Diagram 1) to complete the center square.

Join one burgundy D to one blue-green D as shown (Diagram 2). Repeat to make 15 more D/D triangles. Join pairs of D/D triangles as shown to make 8 D/D squares. Join bright blue Bs to the two burgundy edges of a D/D square (Diagram 3). Repeat to make three more D/B units. Sew a medium gray F to one long edge of each D/B rectangle to complete D/B/F units.

Join blue-gray Bs to burgundy edges of remaining D/D squares. Add a light gray F to one long edge of each D/B unit. (Set this second set of D/B/F units aside for later use.)

Join medium gray Es to bright blue edges of first D/B/F unit (Diagram 4). Repeat to make one more triangle. Join long edges of remaining bright blue D/B/F units to opposite edges of center unit.

Arrange the three sections of the center block as shown and join along long edges to complete the quilt center.

2. Add the inner border. Join a 12" green and a 12" gray strip along one long edge. Repeat to make three more strips. Join strips to the four edges of the quilt center block (Diagram 5).

Instead of adding corner squares to complete the border, appliqué the reserved D/B/F units to fill in the empty space. Turn under the seam allowance on blue and blue-green edges, position the units at corners of border as shown (Diagram 6), pin to secure, and appliqué D/B/F units to border strips.

(Note: There will now be extra layers of fabric on the reverse side of the quilt, under the appliqués. Trim the bottom layer away, leaving ¼" seam allowance.)

Cut gray bias tape into four (13½") lengths. Center lengths of bias tape on outside seams of center block. (Place tape so that the inside edge just covers the seam line.) Beginning at the center and working out toward the edges, slipstitch a piece of bias tape to the quilt top. As you get to the end of the tape, split the seam between the blue-green and burgundy triangles and insert the ends of the tape into the opening (Diagram

7). Slipstitch seams closed. Continue to slipstitch bias tape to remaining edges of center block, overlapping the strips of tape where they meet at the corners and inserting ends into seams.

3. Add the middle border. Stitch a dark green G to each end of one mauve strip. Repeat to make three additional strips. Make a checkerboard block using two blue-green and two burgundy Cs. Repeat to make three additional blocks. Stitch one checkerboard block to each end of a mauve/dark green strip. Repeat to make another border strip.

To add middle border, stitch two mauve/dark green strips to opposite edges of quilt top. Then stitch strips with checkerboard corners to remaining sides (Diagram 8).

4. Add the outer border. Center and stitch one dark green polished cotton strip to one edge of the middle border. Repeat for remaining edges. Miter the corners (Layout Schematic).

Quilting

1. Mark the quilting design. Mark the quilting lines on the quilt top (Quilting Schematic).

2. Stack the layers. Stack the quilt backing (right side down), fleece, and quilt top. Baste securely through all layers. Quilt with white thread.

Trim edges of backing and fleece to match the quilt top.

Finishing

1. Add the piping. Join the burgundy bias strips to make a continuous length. Use bias fabric to make 4½ yards of corded piping. Stitch piping to the right side of the quilt, with piping facing toward center of quilt and stitching line ½″ from edge.

2. Bind the edges. Join dark green bias strips to make a continuous length and use to bind edges of quilt.

Layout Schematic

Diagram 1

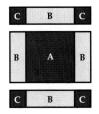

Diagram 2

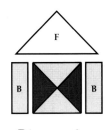

Diagram 3

Diagram 4:
Assembling Center

Diagram 5: Adding Inner Border

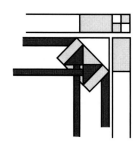

Diagram 8

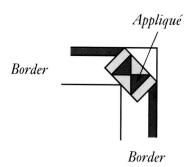

Appliqué

Border

Border

Diagram 6: Appliquéing Corner Piece

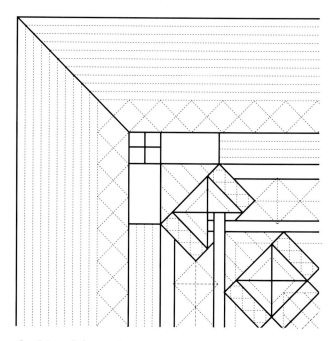

Quilting Schematic
Note: Dotted lines indicate quilting.

Note: All seam allowances are ¹⁄₄".

Open seam here and insert tape.

Diagram 7: Inserting Bias Tape in Corner

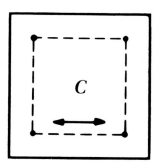

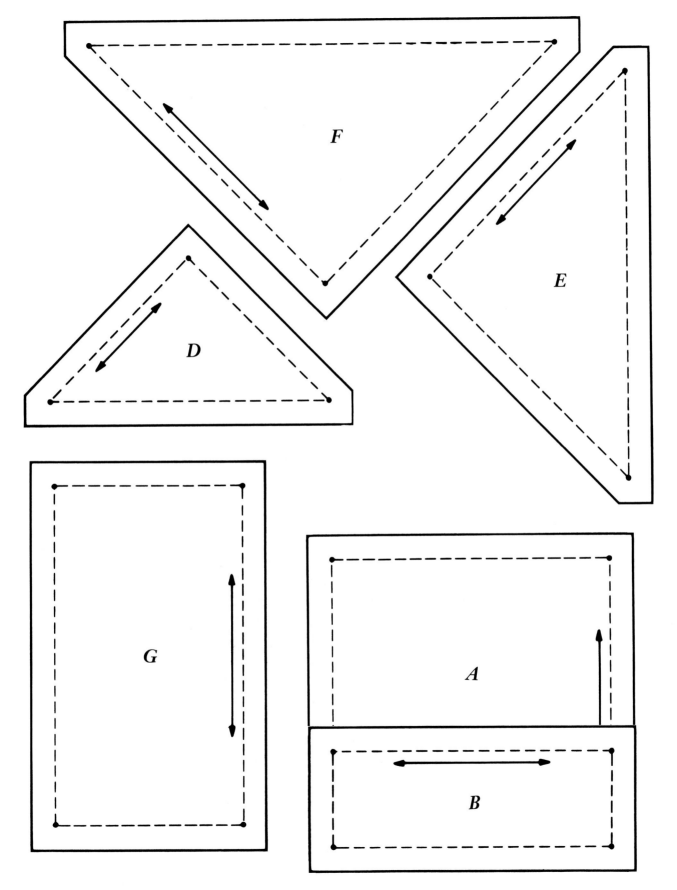

F

E

D

G

A

B

Springtime Stencil

To speed the construction of this picture-perfect quilt, stencil springtime flowers instead of appliquéing them. Each bouquet is framed in a stylized wreath pieced from black and white triangles.

Finished size of quilt: *23¼" x 23¼"*

Number of blocks and finished size: *nine stenciled blocks, 3½" x 3½"; four pieced blocks, 3½" x 3½".*

Materials

White: ⅜ yard
  Pieces to cut: 9 (5" square) for stenciling, 4 (template A), 60 (template B), 9 (template C), 8 (template E), 4 (template F), 24 (template D)

Black print: ½ yard
  Pieces to cut: 120 (template B), 2 (3½" x 17¼") and 2 (3½" x 23¼") for border

Muslin: ¾ yard
  Pieces to cut: 1 (25¼" square) for backing

Polyester fleece: ¾ yard
  Pieces to cut: 1 (23¼" square)

White thread for quilting
Dk. red, green paints
Stenciling supplies

Quilt Top Assembly

Note: All seam allowances are ¼".

1. Make the stenciled blocks. Practice stenciling on scraps of white fabric, using small amounts of paint and a nearly dry brush. When you are satisfied with the results, stencil the design in the center of each 5" block. Center template C over design and trim each block to fit template.

2. Make the pieced blocks. Join one white B and one black B along long edges to make a B/B square. Repeat to make 47 more B/B squares. Join black Bs to the white edges of one B/B square as shown (Diagram 1) to make a B/B triangle. Repeat to make 23 more B/B triangles.

Join long edge of one B/B triangle to one edge of a white A. Repeat, joining B/B triangles to remaining edges of A (Diagram 2) to complete a square. Repeat to make four more A/B squares. Set aside remaining B/B triangles.

Join a black B to a white edge of another B/B square. Join a white D to the remaining white edge as shown (Diagram 3) to make a B/D unit. Repeat, reversing color placement of B and D, to make a mirror-image version of the first B/D unit. Repeat to make 11 more B/D units and 11 more mirror-image B/D units.

To make a corner block, join B/D units to adjacent edges of an F as shown (Diagram 4). Repeat to make three more B/D/F units.

To make an edging block, join one B/B triangle and two B/D units to an E as shown (Diagram 5) to make a B/D/E edging block. Repeat to make seven more.

3. Join the blocks. Join stenciled blocks, pieced whole

blocks, edging blocks, and corner blocks as shown, to assemble rows 1-7 (Diagram 6). Add white Bs as shown to complete each row. Join rows 1-7 to complete pieced center.

4. Add the border. Join 3½" x 17¼" strip to top and bottom edges of center (Layout Schematic). Join remaining 3½" x 23¼" strips to the sides.

Quilting

1. Mark the quilting design. Draw diagonal lines from corner to corner to mark an X through the center of each white A, E, and F.

2. Stack the layers. Stack backing (right side down), fleece, and quilt top. Baste securely through all layers.

3. Quilt. Use white thread to quilt the X in centers of blocks. Also quilt close to the outside edges of every white block and triangle. Trim edges of backing to match quilt top.

Finishing

1. Frame the quilt with a black, 1½"-wide wooden frame.

Diagram 1

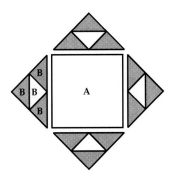

Diagram 2

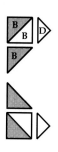

Diagram 3

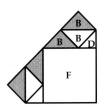

Diagram 4

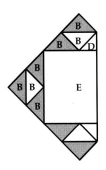

Diagram 5

Layout Schematic

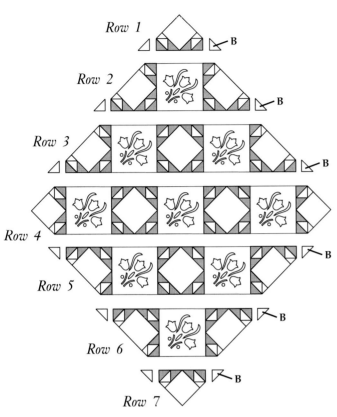

Row 1

B

Row 2

B

Row 3

B

Row 4

B

Row 5

B

Row 6

B

Row 7

B

Diagram 6: Assembling the Top

Note: *All seam allowances are ¹⁄₄".*

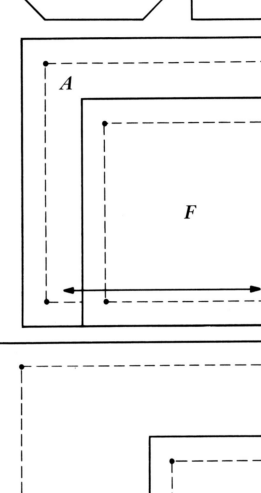

D

B

A

F

C

E

Tulip Stencil Pattern

Fir Trees

*Borrow a trick from Seminole patchwork to piece the small fir trees that
give this quilt its charm. Join light and dark fabric strips,
cut across the stripes to make rows of checks, and then
join the rows to make the precise grid of half-inch squares.*

Finished size of quilt: 38" square

Number of blocks and finished size: nine blocks, 8¼"
x 8¼"

Materials

Dk. green print: ¼ yard
  Pieces to cut: 153" of 1"-wide strips

Lt. green print: ¼ yard
  Pieces to cut: 162" of 1"-wide strips

Lt. tan: ¼ yard
  Pieces to cut: 72" of 1"-wide strips. 18 (template A),
  18 (template C)

Lt. brown: scraps
  Pieces to cut: 9 (template D)

Rust stripe: ⅞ yard
  Pieces to cut: 36 (2½" x 8¾") strips

Lt. tan/rust pindot: ⅜ yard
  Pieces to cut: 24 (1½" x 8¾") strips for sashing

Blue-gray: scraps
  Pieces to cut: 16 (template E)

Gray-green print: ¼ yard
  Pieces to cut: 4 (1½" x 30") strips for border

Lt. tan/navy pindot: 1¾ yards
  Pieces to cut: 4 (3½" x 38") strip for border, 1 (40"
  square) for backing

Gold: 1 yard
  Pieces to cut: 2 (8⅝" square), 4½ yards of 2"-wide
  bias strips for binding

Polyester fleece: 1¼ yards
  Pieces to cut: 1 (38" square)

Tan thread for quilting

Quilt Top Assembly
Note: All seam allowances are ¼".

1. Cut and piece fabric for tree. Cut a 1" square
from one end of a light green fabric strip for row 1.
  To make row 2, cut a 9" length from both the dark
green and the light green print strips. Join the strips
along one long edge. (Note: To prevent unraveling,
machine-stitch seams when using this technique.) Cut
across the band to make a 1"-wide light/dark strip
(Diagram 1).
  To make row 3, repeat the joining and cutting

process, using 2 light green and 2 dark green 9″ strips (Diagram 2). Continue to piece and cut 9″ strips to make rows 4-8, always alternating color, and referring to Diagram 3 for number and placement of strips.

2. Make the tree block. Before joining, lay out all strips for the first tree in rows, to be sure you have pieced them correctly. Then join rows 1 and 2.

Cut a 1¾″ length of light tan fabric strip and join it to the left edge of rows 1 and 2 (Diagram 4). Join rows 3, 4, and 5 to rows 1 and 2 as shown (Diagram 5). Cut a 3″ length of light tan fabric strip and join it to the left edge of the joined strips (Diagram 6).

Cut a 1¾″ length of light tan fabric strip and join it to the right edge of row 7 as shown (Diagram 7). Cut a 3″ length and join it to the right edge of row 8. Join rows 6, 7, and 8 to row 1-5 as shown (Diagram 7) to complete piecing of tree.

Sew a light tan A to each side of the tree top, so that turning dots at corners of As meet intersection of seam allowance on the dark green square at the tree top (Diagram 8).

3. Complete the tree blocks. Place template B over the pieced block, matching top and sides of template with top and sides of As. Mark outline of template on tree portion of block; then cut along outline to trim excess fabric from bottom and sides of tree shape.

Join light tan Cs to sides of a light brown D. Join C/D strip to lower edge of tree block (Diagram 9). Repeat process to make eight more tree blocks.

4. Add the sashing. Center and stitch the 2½″ x 8¾″ striped strips to edges of each tree block. Miter the corners.

Join three tree blocks and four tan/rust pindot strips, alternating blocks and strips. Repeat to make two additional rows of blocks.

Join four blue-gray Es and three tan/rust pindot strips, alternating Es with strips to make a row of sashing. Repeat to make three more rows.

Join rows of blocks and rows of sashing as shown (Diagram 10) to complete the pieced center.

5. Add the border. Join gray-green print strips to right and left edges of the quilt top. Trim off excess fabric. Repeat to join remaining gray-green print strips to top and bottom edges.

Stitch light tan/navy pindot strips to the right and left edges of the quilt top. Trim off excess fabric.

Repeat to join remaining light tan/navy pindot strips to the top and bottom edges.

Fold one 8⅝″ gold square in half diagonally and cut along the fold to make 2 triangles. Repeat for other square.

Fold under ¼″ seam allowance on long edge of each triangle. Place triangles in corners of quilt top as shown (Layout Schematic), matching short edges of triangles to raw edges of quilt top. Appliqué folded edges of triangles to quilt top.

Quilting

1. Mark the quilting design. Mark 2 parallel lines in light tan/navy pindot border (Quilting Schematic). Mark a diagonal grid of 1″ squares in gold corner triangles. Mark quilting lines ¼″ in from seam lines on rust stripe borders of blocks and also down center of border. Mark an undulating line as shown on gray-green print border. Mark remaining lines as shown (Quilting Schematic).

2. Stack the layers. Stack quilt backing (right side down), fleece, and quilt top. Baste securely through all layers.

3. Quilt. Quilt on all marked lines with tan thread. Also quilt next to seam line on all tan fabric in background of tree block and all seam lines of borders and sashing. Quilt parallel lines ½″ apart on tan fabric at base of each tree. Trim edges of backing to match quilt top.

Finishing

1. Bind the edges. Join the gold bias strips to make a continuous length and use it to bind edge of quilt.

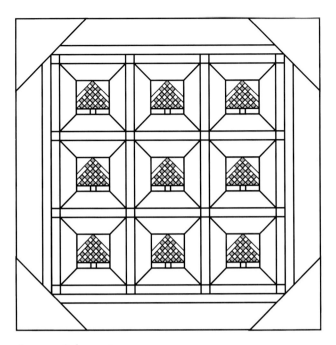

Layout Schematic

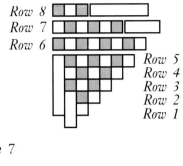

Diagram 7

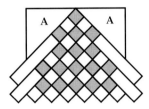

Diagram 8

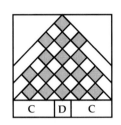

Diagram 9

Diagram 1

Diagram 2

Row 8
Row 7
Row 6
Row 5
Row 4
Row 3
Row 2
Row 1

Diagram 3

Row 1
Row 2

Diagram 4

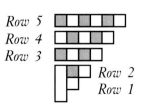

Row 5
Row 4
Row 3
Row 2
Row 1

Diagram 5

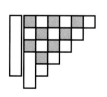

Diagram 6

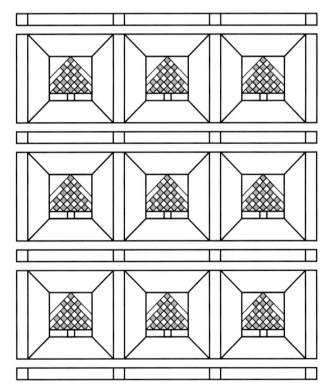

Diagram 10: Assembling Quilt Center

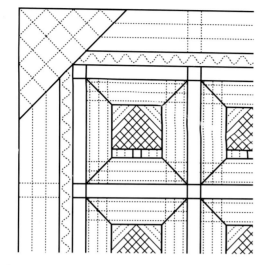

Quilting Schematic
Note: Dotted lines indicate quilting.

Note: All seam allowances are ¼".

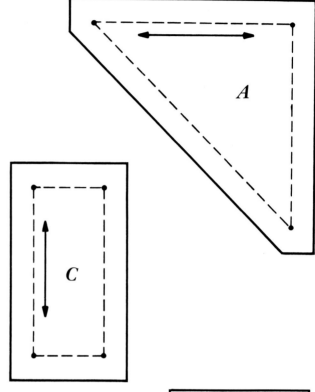

A

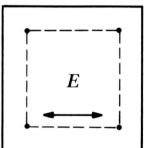

C

E

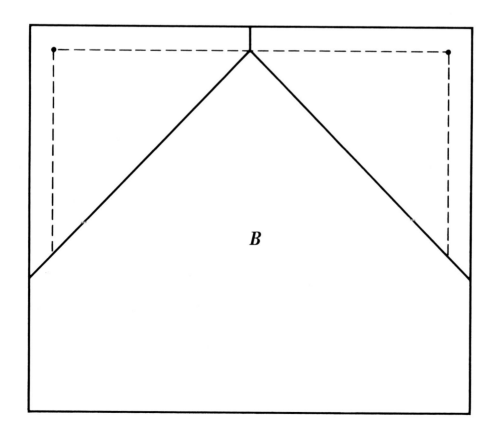

B

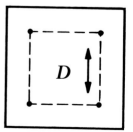

D

Picnic Pair

The next time you pack a country picnic, take along one of these handsome
quilts to spread out under the shade tree. Both designs follow a
basic formula: a checkerboard center framed by two patchwork borders.
Copy these designs or substitute favorite patterns to make your own picnic quilt.

Star Sampler

Quilt Top Assembly

1. Piece the checkerboard center. Match and join long edges of the red print 15" strips and the cream with navy/red print 15" strips, alternating colors. (Note: To prevent unraveling, machine-stitch seams when using this technique.) Cut across the band to divide the pieced strip into 1½"-wide checkered segments. Join segments to make a checkerboard rectangle four squares wide and 10 squares long.

2. Add the sashing. Join a 1½" x 4½" navy print strip to each short edge of the checkerboard center. Stitch a 1½" x 12½" navy print strip to each long edge.

3. Piece the star blocks. Join two matching print Bs to one cream A as shown (Diagram 1). Repeat, using same fabrics, to make three more A/B units.

Join a cream C to each end of one A/B unit. Repeat to make a second strip.

Join remaining A/B units to opposite edges of one D as shown (Diagram 2).

Join A/B/C units to long edges of A/B/D unit as shown (Diagram 3) to complete one star block. Repeat to make nine more star blocks, using a different combination of colors for each.

4. Add the star border. Join one star block to each short edge of the checkerboard center as shown (Diagram 4). Join remaining star blocks to make two rows of four stars each. Join a four-star row to each long edge of checkerboard/star strip.

5. Add the second round of sashing. Join the 18½" navy print strips to top and bottom edges of patchwork panel. Join the 26½" navy print strips to the right and left edges.

6. Piece the Wild Goose border. Join two cream with navy/red print Fs to short edges of a print E to make a Wild Goose block. Repeat to make 45 more E/F units, using cream with navy/red print Fs for all blocks and varying the prints used for the Es to give a random effect.

Join a cream with navy/red print F and an F cut from the assorted prints along long edges to make an F/F square. Repeat to make 15 more F/F units.

Join four F/F squares as shown (Layout Schematic) to make a corner square, arranging the pieces so that the assorted print triangles all point toward the center. Repeat to make three more corner squares.

Join 10 Wild Goose blocks along long edges, with the triangles pointing in the same direction, to make a Wild Goose border strip. Repeat to make another 10-unit strip. Join strips to top and bottom edges of the patchwork panel. Join remaining Wild Goose blocks to make two more strips, each having 13 units. Join a

Wild Goose corner block to each end of each strip. Join strips to right and left edges of patchwork panel.

7. Add the outer border. Join the 28½" navy print strips to top and bottom edges of quilt. Join the 39" navy print strips to the right and left edges to complete quilt top.

Quilting

1. Mark the quilting design. Using quilting templates, mark half-circle motif on all Wild Goose blocks, teardrop motif on all Star blocks, and continuous swirl motif on inner and outer borders. (See Quilting Schematic for placement.) Mark the corner motifs for the wide border free-hand, using corner design for narrow borders as a guide.

Mark diagonal lines from corner to corner within each checkerboard square. Fill in cream print background of star blocks with parallel lines about ⅜" apart. Fill in background of Wild Goose block with the same pattern.

2. Stack the layers. Stack the quilt backing (right side down), the fleece, and the quilt top. Baste securely through all layers.

3. Quilt. Quilt along all marked lines, using red thread. Trim edges of backing and fleece to match quilt top.

Finishing

1. Bind the edges. Join the strips of red print bias fabric to make a continuous length and use to bind edges of quilt.

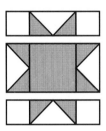

Diagram 3

Layout Schematic

Diagram 1

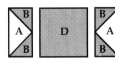

Diagram 2

Diagram 4

Quilting Schematic
Note: Dotted lines indicate quilting.

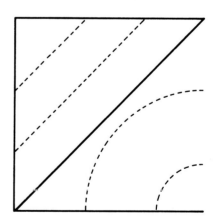

Wide Border Quilting Pattern

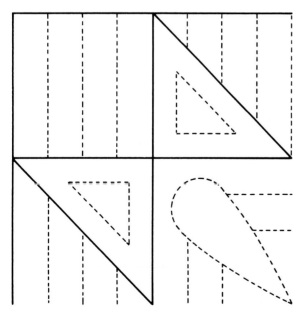

Star Block Quilting Pattern
Note: This is ¼ of design.

Wild Goose Block Quilting Pattern
Note: This is ½ of design.

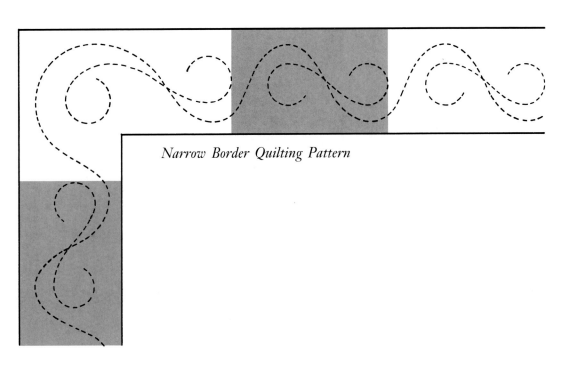

Narrow Border Quilting Pattern

Note: All seam allowances are ¹/₄".

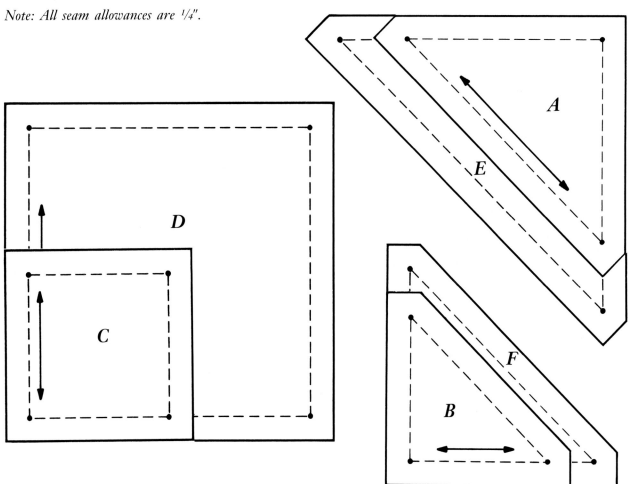

Churn Dash

Quilt Top Assembly
Note: All seam allowances are ¼".

1. Piece the checkerboard center. Join the 12" navy plaid and 12" polka-dot strips along long edges, alternating fabrics to make a light-and-dark-striped band of fabric. (Note: To prevent unraveling, machine-stitch seams when using this technique.) Cut across the band to divide it into 1½"-wide checkered segments. Join the strips to make the checkerboard center, eight squares wide and eight squares long.

2. Add the inner border. Stitch 1½" x 8½" navy strips to top and bottom edges of the checkerboard center. Add 1½" x 10½" navy strips to sides.

3. Make the Churn Dash blocks. Join a red windowpane A and a white/cream A along one long edge to make an A/A square. Repeat to make 15 more red/white A/A units.

Join navy plaid As to white/cream As to make 16 additional squares.

Join navy windowpane As to white/cream As to make a third set of 16 squares. Set aside the three sets of A/A units.

Join a 3" x 18" white/cream strip on either side of the 1½" x 18" navy strip. Cut band into 12 (1½"-wide) white/navy/white strips. Set aside.

Stitch a red windowpane/white A/A square to either side of one white B (Diagram 1). Repeat to make one more A/B rectangle.

Join A/B rectangles to long edges of one white/navy/white strip, as shown, to complete a Churn Dash block. Repeat to make three additional red/white Churn Dash blocks, four navy windowpane/white Churn Dash blocks, and four navy plaid/white Churn Dash blocks.

4. Make the Churn Dash border. Lay out color sequence for Churn Dash blocks as desired, placing red/white blocks on corners. Join two blocks for the top row, two blocks for the bottom, and two rows of four blocks each for the sides. Join the two-block rows to top and bottom edges of center section (Diagram 2). Join four-block rows to the sides.

5. Add the middle border. Join the 1½" x 20½" navy strips to top and bottom edges of Churn Dash center. Join the 1½" x 22½" navy strips to the sides (Layout Schematic).

6. Add the Sawtooth border. Join a polka-dot A to an A cut from one of the assorted prints, to make an A/A Sawtooth square. Repeat to make 47 more A/A squares.

Arranging the colors of the squares at random, join units to make two (13-block) Sawtooth rows and two (11-block) Sawtooth rows.

With the polka-dot triangles on the outside edge, join 11-block Sawtooth borders to top and bottom edges (Layout Schematic). Join 13-block borders to the sides.

7. Add the outer border. Join the 2¾″ x 26½″ navy strips to top and bottom edges of the quilt. Join 2¾″ x 31″ navy strips to the sides.

Quilting

1. Mark the quilting design. Draw diagonal lines from corner to corner to mark an X in each square of the checkerboard center. Mark a diagonal grid of ¼″ squares on the white/cream print background of each Churn Dash block as shown (Quilting Schematic). Mark diagonal lines ⅜″ apart to cover the white background of the Sawtooth border. Mark border lines, referring to Quilting Schematic for placement. Trace Border Quilting Pattern in borders as shown.

2. Stack the layers. Stack quilt backing (right side down), fleece, and quilt top. Baste securely through all layers.

3. Quilt. Quilt on marked lines with red thread. Outline quilt ¼″ inside seam lines on dark triangles with red thread. Trim backing and fleece to match top.

Finishing

1. Bind the edges. Join navy check bias strips to make a continuous length and use to bind edges of quilt.

Layout Schematic

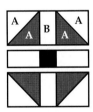

Diagram 1

Diagram 2

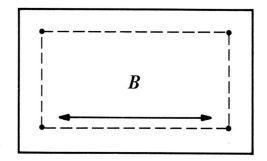

Note: *All seam allowances are ¼".*

B

Quilting Schematic

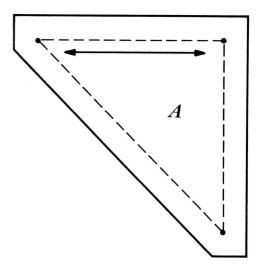

A

Border Quilting Pattern

Iris

*Like a springtime garden captured in stained glass, these geometric
blossoms glow with luminous color. Fine quilting shrinks
the background fabric just a bit, causing the lightly quilted blossoms
to puff up as if they had been carefully stuffed.*

Quilt Top Assembly

Note: All seam allowances are ¼".

1. Piece the iris block. Join a magenta A to a yellow B. Join the A/B unit to a rose C (Diagram 1). Join a white A to a purple D as shown (Diagram 2). Make a second A/D unit by joining a white A to a magenta D, reversing the pieces so that the second A/D unit is a mirror image of the first. Join the purple A/D to the left edge of the A/B/C unit and the magenta A/D unit to the right edge to complete upper half of iris block.

Join a white E to each long diagonal edge of a purple F (Diagram 3). Add lavender Gs to the upper right and upper left diagonal edges as shown, to complete lower half of iris block.

Join upper half of iris to lower half of iris as shown (Diagram 4). (You may find it easier to stitch this seam by hand.)

Join one lavender H to one white I to make left side of the iris block. Make a mirror-image H/I set for the right side of the block. Add H/I strips to iris unit to complete the iris block. Repeat to make 2 more iris blocks.

2. Piece the leaf blocks. Join one green J to one white K. Join a green H to the right edge of the J/K unit (Diagram 5). Join a white L to the bottom edge to complete the leaf block (Diagram 6). Repeat to make one more. Make two more leaf blocks that are mirror-images of the first two.

3. Piece the quilt top. Use template M to trace seam lines onto the back of each white M, and each leaf block. Draw seam lines on each iris block ¼" in from cut edge. (Note: Each iris block is twice as wide as an M block.) Join plain, iris, and leaf blocks in rows, by sewing side seams from corner dot to corner dot (Diagram 7). Backstitch at both ends of the stitching.

For row 1, join two white Ms along long edges, stitching from corner dot to corner dot. Repeat to make another M/M pair. Join one pair of Ms to the left edge of an iris block and one pair to the right edge to complete row 1 (Layout Schematic).

For row 2, join one M, one iris block, one leaf block and a pair of Ms.

For row 3, stitch together one pair of Ms, one leaf block, one iris block and one M.

For row 4, stitch together one M, one leaf block, another M, another leaf block, and a pair of Ms (Layout Schematic).

Join rows 1 and 2, stitching from dot to dot and leaving diamond-shaped openings where corners of blocks meet (Diagram 8). Clip seam allowances of Cs at top of Iris blocks to the corner dots. Fold under seam allowances of the diamond-shaped openings, slide N pieces under the openings, and reverse-appliqué Ns to quilt top. (See photo for color placement.) Turn quilt top to wrong side and trim extra fabric from corners of white blocks, leaving ¼″ seam allowances. In a similar manner, fill in notches around the edges of the quilt top by reverse-appliquéing Os in the V-shaped openings and Ps in the corners. (See photo for color placement.) Trim extra fabric from corners of white blocks as before.

4. Add the border. Join the blue strips to the white strips, matching edges. Center and stitch one border strip to one long edge of the quilt top. Repeat procedure on remaining edges. Miter the corners. Trim seam allowances on mitered seams to ¼″.

5. Embroider the stems. Satin-stitch iris stems, using two strands of lavender floss, and stitching directly over the seam line.

Quilting

1. Mark the quilting design. Mark outline quilting ¼″ inside seam lines on all M pieces. On remaining pieces, mark outline quilting ¼″ inside seam lines joining block to block, on white fabric only. Mark a ½″ diamond grid inside lines just marked. Continue quilting pattern from background of quilt into border, including the "seam lines" to give an illusion of pieced M blocks.

2. Stack the layers. Stack the backing (right side down), batting, and top. Baste securely through all layers.

3. Quilt. Quilt on all marked lines with white thread. Also quilt in-the-ditch inside each blue diamond and on both edges of the blue border. Quilt close to the seam of all leaves and green diamonds with green thread. Quilt close to seam in all iris pieces with purple thread. Trim edges of quilt backing to match quilt top.

Finishing

1. Bind the edges. Join strips of light green bias fabric to make a continuous length. Use to bind edges of quilt.

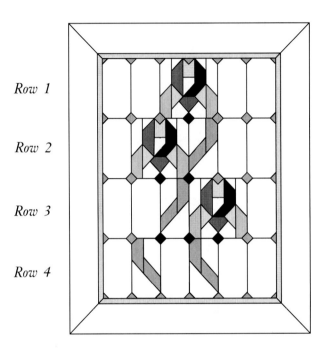

Row 1

Row 2

Row 3

Row 4

Layout Schematic

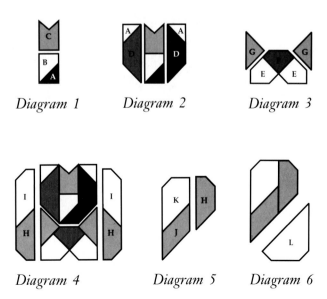

Diagram 1   *Diagram 2*   *Diagram 3*

Diagram 4   *Diagram 5*   *Diagram 6*

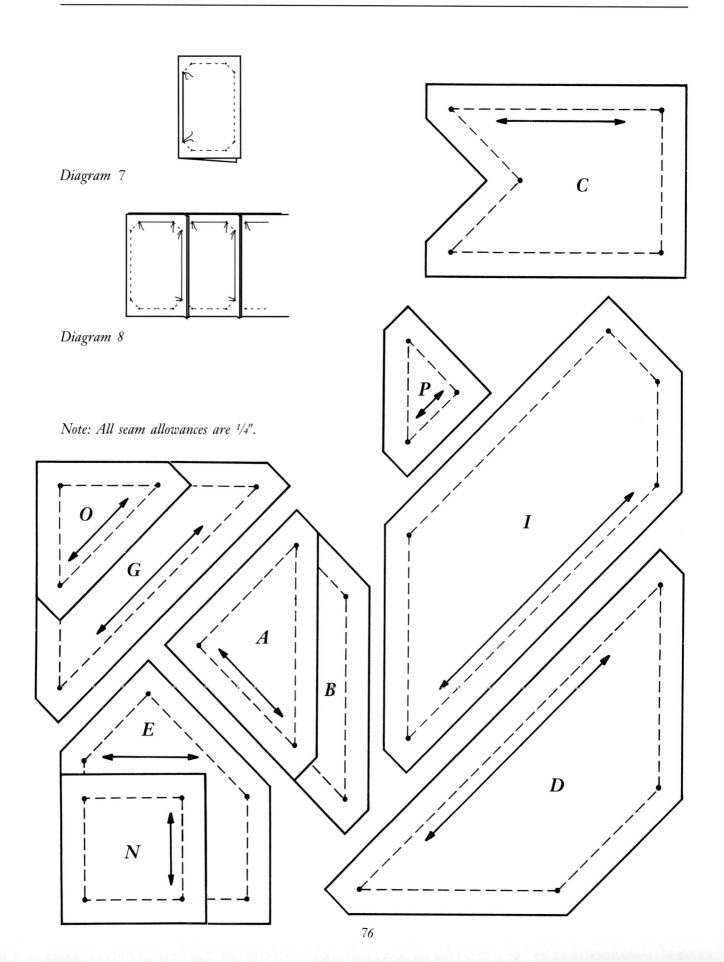

Diagram 7

Diagram 8

Note: *All seam allowances are ¹/₄".*

C

P

O

G

I

A

B

D

E

N

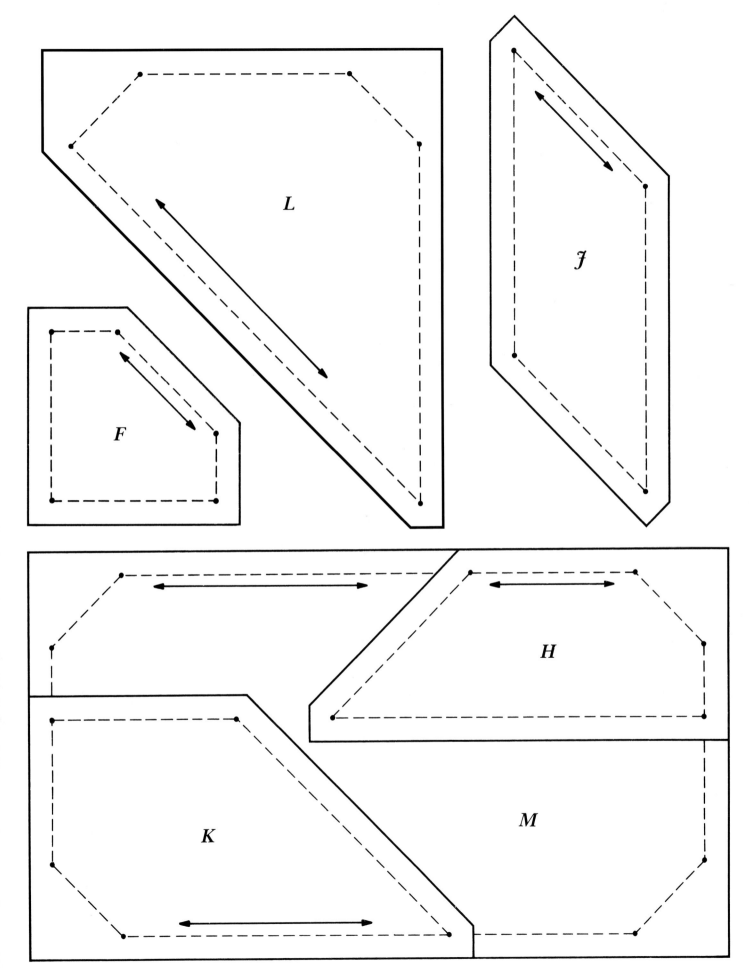

Patriotic Pride

The perfect size for a centerpiece on a festive table, this quilt design plays with lights and darks to create the illusion of a diamond set on point within a square. Triple borders make a handsome frame for the geometric patchwork.

Finished size of quilt: 23" x 23"

Materials

Navy plaid: ⅛ yard
  Pieces to cut: 8 (template A), 8 (template C)

Muslin: ⅛ yard
  Pieces to cut: 8 (template A), 4 (template B)

Tan: ⅜ yard
  Pieces to cut: 8 (template E), 4 (1½" x 25") for border

White print: ⅛ yard
  Pieces to cut: 4 (template F)

Navy print: 1¼ yards
  Pieces to cut: 1 (template F), 4 (template D), 4 (2½" x 25") for border, 1 (25" square) for backing, 2½ yards of 2"-wide bias strips for binding

Red print: ⅛ yard
  Pieces to cut: 4 (1" x 25") for border

Polyester fleece: ¾ yard
  Pieces to cut: 2 (23" square)

Red, tan thread for quilting

Quilt Top Assembly

Note: All seam allowances are ¼".

1. Piece the center. Join one navy plaid A to each short edge of one muslin B (Diagram 1). Repeat to make three more A/B units. Set aside.

Join muslin As to two adjacent edges of one plaid C to make an A/C triangle. Join long edge of the triangle to long edge of a navy print D (Diagram 2). Repeat to make three more squares. Set aside.

Join an E to each end of an A/B rectangle as shown (Diagram 3). Join a C to each E to complete row 1 of quilt center. Repeat to make row 5.

Join A/C/D squares to right and left edges of a white print F as shown. Join an E to each end of this strip to complete row 2. Repeat to make row 4.

Join a white print F to right and left edges of a navy print F. Join an A/B unit to each end of this strip to complete row 3.

Join rows 1-5 as shown to complete quilt center.

2. Add the borders. Join one red print strip, one tan strip, and one navy print strip on long edges. Repeat to make three additional strips. Center and stitch one strip to top edge of quilt center. Repeat for three remaining edges (Layout Schematic). Miter the corners. Trim seam allowance to ¼" on mitered seams.

Quilting

1. Mark the quilting design. Mark diagonal lines ½" apart in each tan E, making sure quilting lines are parallel to the center diamond outlined by white As and Bs. Trace quilting design in each F block (Quilting Schematic).

2. Layer the quilt. Layer the quilt backing (right side down), the two layers of fleece, and the quilt top. Baste securely through all layers.

3. Quilt. Quilt on all lines inside diamond area with red thread. Outline-quilt ¼″ from seams of muslin As and navy plaid Cs with red thread.

Quilt all remaining lines with tan thread. Outline-quilt ¼″ from seams of navy print Ds, navy plaid As, and remaining navy plaid Cs. Also quilt in-the-ditch of each border strip. Trim backing and fleece to match quilt top.

Finishing

1. Bind the edges. Join navy print bias strips to make a continuous length and use to bind edges of quilt.

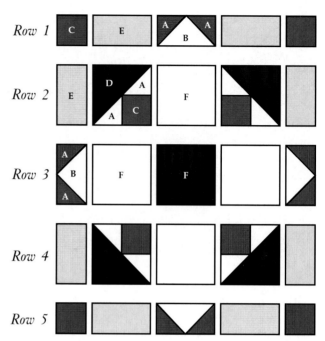

Diagram 3: Assembling Quilt Center

Layout Schematic

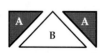

Diagram 1

Diagram 2

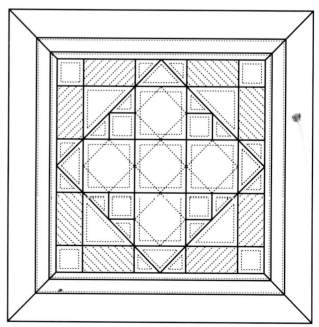

Quilting Schematic
Note: Dotted lines indicate quilting lines.

Note: *All seam allowances are ¹/₄".*

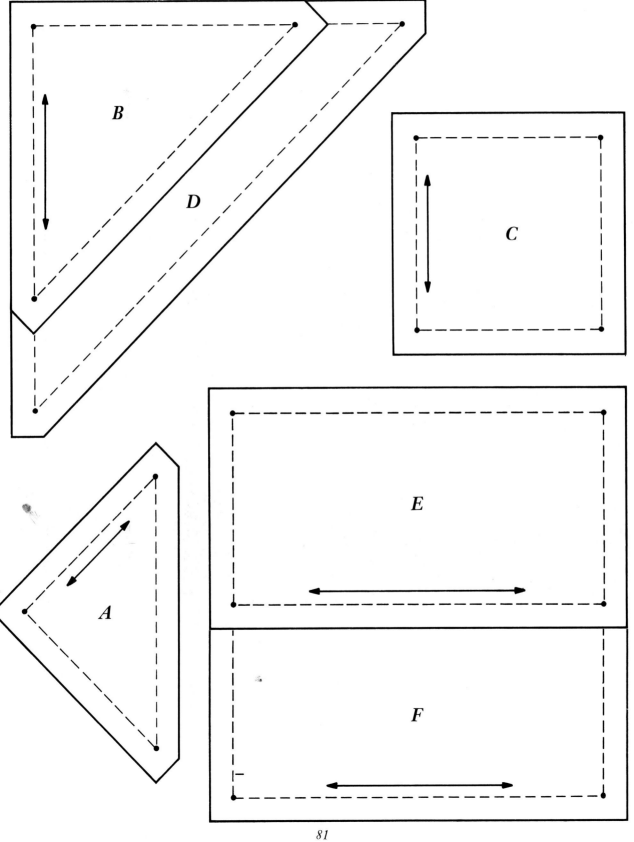

Oriental Fans

With only three pattern pieces and no quilting at all, this richly textured fan design is as timesaving as it is sophisticated. Antique buttons tie the layers together, and liberal use of ribbons in the appliqués means fewer edges to turn under.

Finished size of quilt: 27½" x 27½"

Number of blocks and finished size: nine (6" x 6") for center; 28 (3" x 3") for border

Materials

Muslin: 1 yard
  Pieces to cut: 46 (3½" square)

Olive taffeta: ⅜ yard
  Pieces to cut: 6 (template A), 8 (template B)

Cream faille: ¼ yard
  Pieces to cut: 3 (template A), 7 (template B)

Black satin: ⅛ yard
  Pieces to cut: 8 (template B)

Black faille: 1 yard
  Pieces to cut: 4 (template B), 1 (31½" square) for backing and self-binding

Flannel: 1 yard
  Pieces to cut: 1 (27" square)

Appliqué materials for fans: scraps
  Pieces to cut: 185 (4"-long) strips of fabric and ribbon in widths ranging from 1" to 4".

Note: Appliqué materials on the quilt shown include black satin ribbon, grosgrain ribbon, metallic dot and stripe ribbons, black satin fabric, and moiré taffeta fabric.

Metallic gold thread for couching
Black thread for couching
21 antique metal buttons of various sizes
Two to four buckles or pieces of beaded trim

Quilt Top Assembly
Note: All seam allowances are ¼".

1. Piece the fan blocks. All fan strips are appliquéd to 3½" muslin squares. Place template C (fan) on a square as shown (Diagram 1). Mark the curved top edge of the fan and the turning dot at the base on the muslin square. Repeat to mark remaining squares. Use these markings to guide you when placing the strips. (Note:

There will be three to five appliquéd strips per fan, depending on the width of the strips used.)

Place first fabric strip on the muslin as shown (Diagram 2), matching one long edge of strip with left edge of fan. Pin to secure.

Fold under ¼" seam allowance on the left edge of a second strip and overlap the first strip with the second as shown (Diagram 3). Note that the left edge of the second strip intersects the dot at base of fan and

touches right edge of first strip on the curved line at the top. Slipstitch left edge of second strip to first strip. To reduce bulk, trim excess material from first strip before applying the third strip. (Note: If you are using ribbon instead of fabric, there is no need to turn under a seam allowance on slipstitched edges.)

Continue to add strips as needed to cover the fan, making sure that all strips intersect at the dot and completely cover the curved line at the top of fan (Diagram 4).

When all strips have been appliquéd, place template C over the appliqués on the muslin square. Mark and trim along the cutting line (Diagram 5).

2. Piece the quilt top. To make the nine center blocks, join two fan pieces to make a C/C unit. Fold under seam allowance on the curved edge of one A, clipping the seam allowance at regular intervals to smooth the curve. Slipstitch the A piece to the C/C unit. Repeat to make eight more large fan blocks.

To piece small blocks for the border, match Bs to remaining single fan blocks. Fold under seam allowance on curved edge of each B, clip seam allowances, and slipstitch the Bs to the Cs to make 28 small fan blocks.

Join the large fan blocks to make three rows of three blocks each. Join the rows to assemble the center section (Diagram 6). Make two rows of six small fan blocks each and join to the right and left edges of the quilt top (Diagram 7).Make two rows of eight small fan blocks each. Join these rows to the top and bottom edges.

Where black fabric or ribbon meets black, use black thread to couch gold thread to seam lines to accent the fan shapes.

3. Add the backing and binding. Find and mark center of the back/binding piece, the flannel, and the quilt top by folding each piece into quarters. Stack the back/binding (right side down), flannel, and quilt top, matching centers and keeping edges parallel. Baste through all layers to secure.

Fold 2″ of back/binding to front of quilt top as shown in Layout Schematic, overlapping top edge of quilt. Fold under raw edge of backing ¼″, to make a 1¾″-wide self-binding. Slipstitch binding to quilt top. (To keep binding smooth, begin in center of each strip and work out to the edges.)

Finishing

1. Add the buttons. Sew buttons on at circles as shown (Layout Schematic), stitching through all layers. Stitch small buckles and pieces of beading to the quilt as desired for additional embellishment.

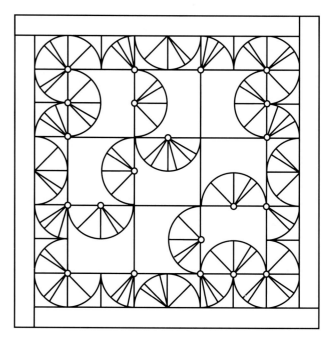

Layout Schematic

Diagram 1

Diagram 2

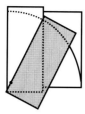

Diagram 3

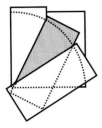

Diagram 4

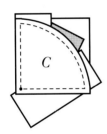

Diagram 5

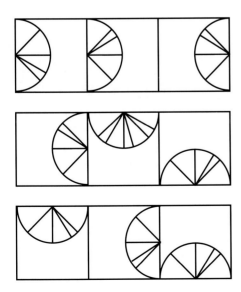

Diagram 6: Assembling the Center

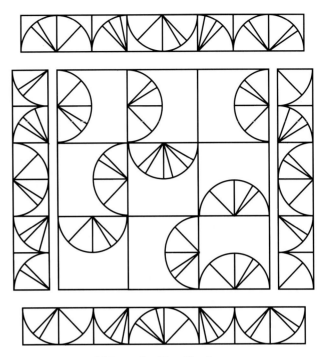

Diagram 7: Adding the Fan Border

Note: All seam allowances are ¼".

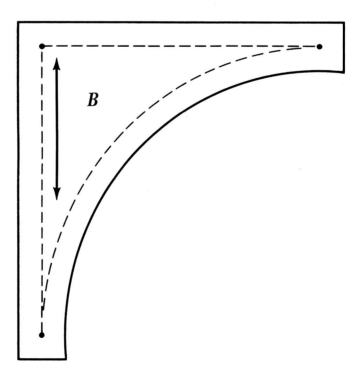

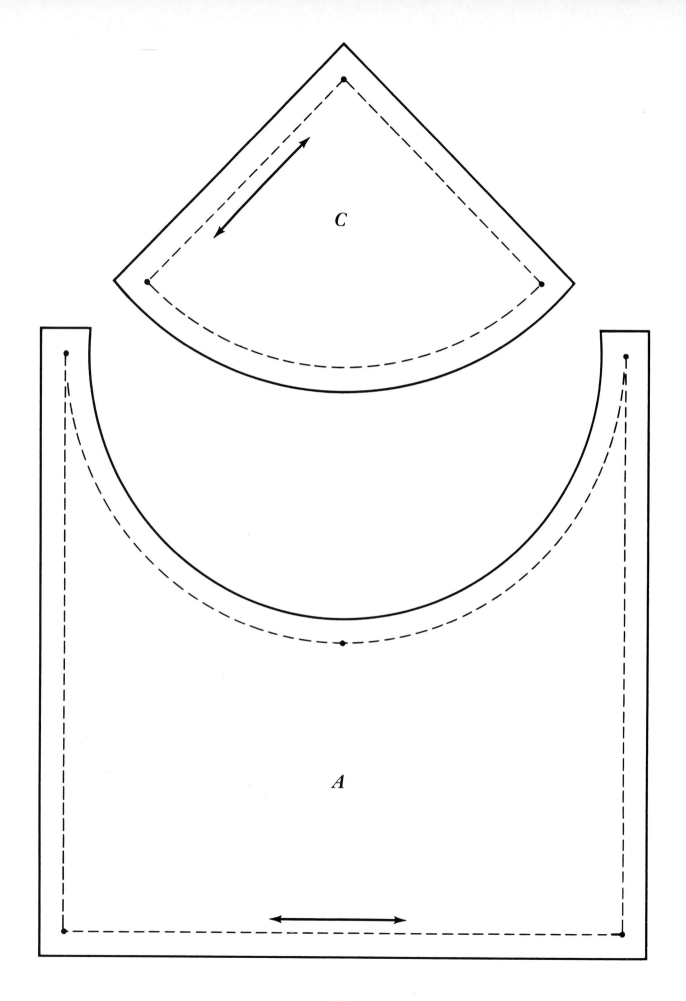

C

A

86

O Christmas Tree

The size of this Christmas hanging makes it a good choice to replace a favorite painting or poster, just in time for the holidays. Quilt sashing doubles as window sashing in the simple-to-piece design.

<table>
<tr><td>

Finished size of quilt: 27" x 33"

Number of blocks and finished size: 12 blocks, each 5" x 5"

Materials

Dk. red print: 1/8 yard
  Pieces to cut: 4 (template A), 4 (template A)*

Sage green print: 1/4 yard
  Pieces to cut: 2 (template C), 6 (template E), 3 (template D), 2 (template B), 2 (template J), 2 (template J), 2 (template I), 2 (template H), 2 (5 1/2" square piece K)*

Dk. green print: 1/4 yard
  Pieces to cut: 2 (template B), 1 (template D), 1 (template G), 3 (template J), 3 (template J), 14 (template E)*

Tan/green pindot: 1 1/2 yards
  Pieces to cut: 1 (29" x 35") for backing, 2 (2" x 35") and 2 (2" x 29") for border, 3 (2" x 18 1/2") for sashing, 8 (2" x 5 1/2") for sashing

Dk. green/red pindot: 1 yard
  Pieces to cut: 5 (template F), 2 (3" x 35") and 2 (3" x 29") for border, 3 1/2 yards of 1 1/4"-wide bias strips for binding

Polyester fleece: 3/4 yard
  Pieces to cut: 1 (27" x 33") piece

Red, dk. green thread for quilting

Note: *Flip or reverse template if fabric is one-sided.*

</td></tr>
</table>

Quilt Top Assembly

Note: All seam allowances are 1/4".

1. Piece row 1. Begin with the star block at the center of row 1 (Diagram 1). Join one red print A and one A* along one long edge as shown (Diagram 2). Repeat to make three more A/A units.

Join one sage print B to one dark green B. Repeat to make another B/B unit. Join one red print A unit to a sage/dark green B/B unit, to make an A/B unit for lower left corner of star. Repeat to make a second A/B unit for lower right corner of star. (Note that the second A/B unit is a mirror-image of the first.)

Join a sage C to each remaining A unit to make 2 A/C units. Join one A/C unit to one A/B unit as shown (Diagram 3). Join remaining A/C unit to remaining A/B unit. (Note that the second A/B/A/C unit is a mirror-image of the first.) Join the two A/B/A/C units.

Join the dark green print D to the lower edge of star. Join the three sage Ds to sides and top of star to complete star block.

2. Piece the squares for rows 2-4. Join one sage print J to one dark green print E (Diagram 1, row 2, left side). Repeat to make one more J/E unit. Join the two J/E units to complete square for left side of row 2. Repeat, using J* to make a mirror-image square for right side.

To make center square, join two dark green print Es to one dark green pindot F. Repeat to make one more E/F unit. Join the E/F units as shown to complete the center square.

For row 3, join one sage print E to one dark green print J (Diagram 1, row 3 left side). Repeat to make one more. Join the two E/J units to complete left square. Repeat, using J* to make mirror-image square for the right side.

Make center square same as for row 2.

For row 4, make an E/J unit as for row 3. Join it to a sage I as shown to complete the left square. Repeat, using J* to make a mirror-image square for the right side. To make center square, make one E/F unit as for rows 2 and 3. Join Hs to right and left edges of a G. Join E/F unit to H/G unit as shown, to complete square.

3. Add the sashing. Join squares for row 1, with sage Ks on either side of star block as shown (Layout Schematic), and with 5 1/2" tan sashing strips between blocks. Join remaining rows as shown. Join rows 1-4 with 18½″ tan sashing strips.

4. Add the border. Match one dark green pindot strip to one tan/green pindot strip. Join along one long edge. Repeat to make two 35″ border units and two 29″ border units.

Center and join a 35″ border unit to one long edge of quilt top. Repeat for remaining long edge. Join 29″ border units to top and bottom edges of quilt. Miter the corners (Layout Schematic).

Quilting

1. Mark the quilting design. Mark the poinsettia quilting pattern in each corner of border.

2. Stack the layers. Stack the quilt backing (right side down), fleece, and quilt top. Baste securely through all layers.

3. Quilt. With red thread, quilt ¼″ inside and outside of star seam line, and outside the outline of the tree. Use red thread to echo-quilt with lines ¼″ apart on Bs and Cs surrounding star and on green pindot pieces inside tree. Use green thread to quilt two rows ¼″ apart on the green pindot border, next to tan pindot sashing. Quilt in-the-ditch around each 5″ x 5″ block and on all other quilting lines with green thread. Trim edges of quilt backing and fleece to match quilt top.

Finishing

1. Bind the edges. Join the dk. green/red pindot bias strips to make a continuous length and use to bind edges of quilt.

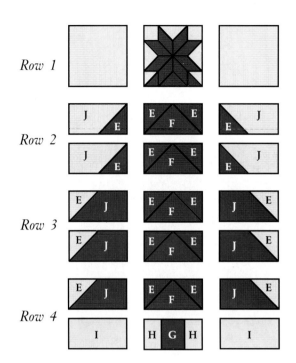

Diagram 1: Assembling the Five-Inch Squares

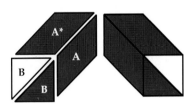

Diagram 2

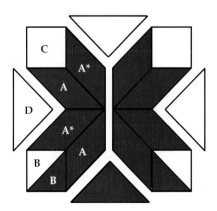

Diagram 3

Layout Schematic

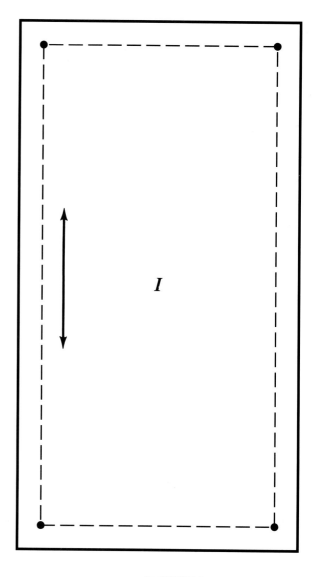

I

Poinsettia Quilting Pattern

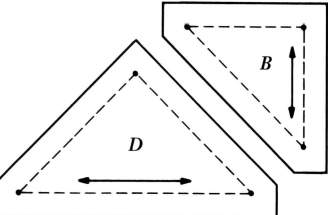

B

D

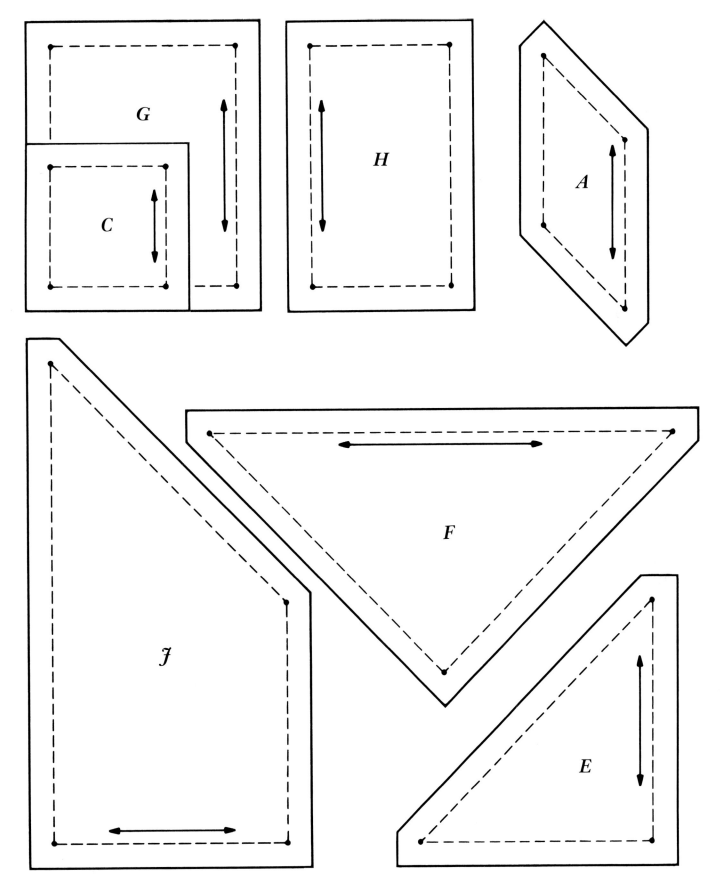

Autumn Leaves

Fabric leaves flutter and float across this jewel-tone hanging to copy the
subtle ways of Mother Nature—no two blocks are exactly alike.
Differences in color and positioning add a richness to the design and make
the piecing challenging enough to hold the interest
of experienced quilters.

Finished size of quilt: *18" x 27"*

Number of blocks and finished size: 15 blocks, each
4" x 4"

Materials

Yellow: scraps
  Pieces to cut: 4 (template A), 2 (template B)

Tan: scraps
  Pieces to cut: 8 (template A), 3 (template B),
  2 (template C)

Gold: scraps
  Pieces to cut: 9 (template A), 3 (template B),
  3 (template C)

Cinnamon: scraps
  Pieces to cut: 3 (template A), 3 (template C)

Rust: 1¼ yards
  Pieces to cut: 6 (template A), 3 (template B), 2 (2" x
  20") and 2 (2" x 29") for border, 1 (20" x 29") for
  backing, 2¾ yards of 2"-wide bias strips for binding

Burgundy: scraps
  Pieces to cut: 3 (template A), 3 (template C)

Very lt. blue: scraps
  Pieces to cut: 3 (template B), 4 (template C),
  1 (template E), 2 (template F)

Lt. blue: ⅛ yard
  Pieces to cut: 7 (template B), 6 (template C),
  2 (template D), 2 (template E), 4 (template F)

Med. blue: ⅛ yard
  Pieces to cut: 7 (template B), 7 (template C),
  6 (template D), 5 (template F)

Blue: ⅛ yard
  Pieces to cut: 9 (template B), 16 (template C),
  3 (template D), 3 (template E), 4 (template F)

Dk. blue: ⅛ yard
  Pieces to cut: 4 (template B), 11 (template C),
  1 (template D), 4 (template E), 2 (template F)

Navy: ⅜ yard
  Pieces to cut: 12 (1" x 4½") and 2 (1" x 22½") for
  sashing, 2 (1" x 20") and 2 (1" x 29") for border

Polyester fleece: ¾ yard
  Pieces to cut: 1 (18" x 27")

Gold, rust, and navy embroidery floss to match fabrics
  for quilting and for leaf stems.

Quilt Top Assembly

Note: All seam allowances are ¼". Since all templates are 1½"-wide, you can save time by cutting long 1½"-wide strips and then marking and cutting strips to produce pattern pieces as needed. Close inspection of the photo will reveal that the leaf blocks have been pieced in several different ways. To simplify piecing, we have adapted instructions to produce the same effect by repeating a single block pattern.

1. Piece the blocks. Note: To avoid confusion, piece the first block from start to finish; then go on to complete each block as shown, instead of doing step 1 for all blocks and going on to step 2, as you might when making a simpler quilt.

Begin by assembling the top block in row 1, referring to Diagram 1 for colors and placement of pieces. Join a dark blue C and a tan C along long edges to make a C/C square (Diagram 2). Join a yellow B to the square to make a B/C rectangle.

Join a blue C to a yellow A as shown (Diagram 3).

Join the B/C rectangle to the left edge of the C/A rectangle to make a square.

Join a blue C to a yellow A as shown (Diagram 4). Join the C/A rectangle to the right edge of the square to make a large rectangle.

Join a blue C to a tan A as shown (Diagram 5). Join a dark blue B to the right edge of the C/A unit to make a strip. Join the strip to the lower edge of the large rectangle to complete the leaf unit.

(Note: All leaf units will be assembled in the same way although the colors used for each block will be different. Refer to Diagram 1 for color and placement of pieces when constructing remaining leaf units.)

To complete the first leaf block, join a blue E to the right edge of the leaf unit as shown (Diagram 1). Join a dark blue F to the lower edge.

Make 15 more blocks, referring to Diagram 1 for color and placement of pieces.

2. Add the sashing. When all blocks are completed, arrange the blocks in 3 vertical rows as shown (Diagram 1). Join one navy 1" x 4½" strip to the bottom edge of each of the top four blocks in rows 1-3. Stitch the five blocks of each row together to make three vertical rows. Join the rows with the navy 1" x 22½" strips between.

3. Add the border. Join the remaining navy strips to the rust strips, matching lengths. Center and join 29" navy/rust strips to sides of quilt and 20" strips to top and bottom edges. Miter the corners.

4. Embroider the stems. Mark placement for each stem (Layout and Quilting Schematic). Outline-stitch with two strands of floss, using gold floss for the yellow/tan and gold/cinnamon leaves and rust floss for the rust/burgundy leaves.

Quilting

1. Mark the quilting design. On all of the blue background, mark horizontal lines ¼" apart. On all leaves, mark ¼" inside edges of leaf; then fill space with horizontal lines ¼" apart. Trace Leaf Quilting Pattern onto border.

2. Stack the layers. Stack the quilt backing (right side down), fleece, and quilt top. Baste securely through all layers.

3. Quilt. Quilt the background with 1 strand navy floss. Quilt the yellow/tan/gold/cinnamon leaves with gold floss. Quilt the rust/burgundy leaves with rust floss. Quilt in-the-ditch around all sashing with navy floss. Quilt the leaf pattern in the border with rust floss. Trim edges of backing and fleece to match the quilt top.

Finishing

1. Bind the edges. Join rust bias strips to make a continuous length and use to bind edges of quilt.

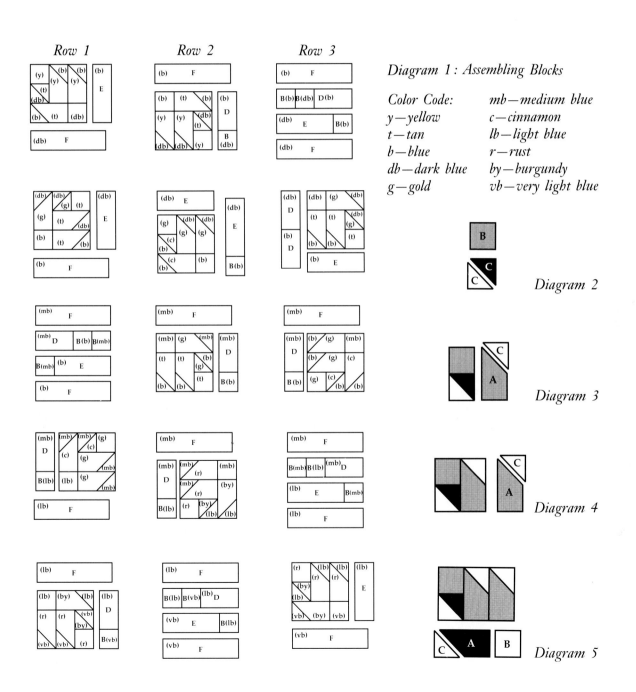

Row 1   *Row 2*   *Row 3*

Diagram 1: Assembling Blocks

Color Code:
y — yellow
t — tan
b — blue
db — dark blue
g — gold

mb — medium blue
c — cinnamon
lb — light blue
r — rust
by — burgundy
vb — very light blue

Diagram 2

Diagram 3

Diagram 4

Diagram 5

Layout and Quilting Schematic
Note: Dotted lines indicate quilting.

Leaf Quilting Pattern

Note: All seam allowances are ¼".

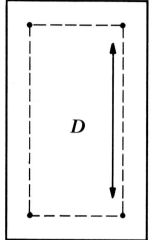

D

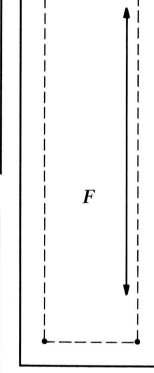

F

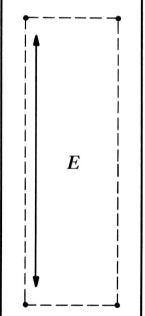

E

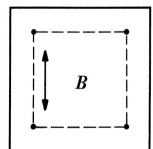

B

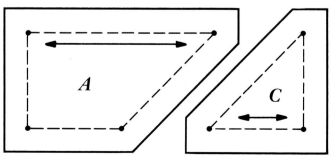

A

C

Summer Flowers

Stitch a dozen patchwork flowers for a cool summer quilt that's laid out like a formal garden and surrounded by a pieced garden wall. Or make just one blossom for a tailored pillow.

Quilt Top Assembly

Note: All seam allowances are ¼".

1. Piece the poppy corner blocks. Join one light green A and one blue A. Join a light blue A to each edge of blue A (Diagram 1). Join a purple B to the A/A triangle to complete the poppy flower.

To make leaf sections, join one light green A to one dark green C. Make mirror-image A/C unit with one light green A and one aqua C (Diagram 2). Join A/C unit to light green D; repeat to make mirror-image unit. Join A/C/D unit to aqua E; repeat for mirror-image unit, using dark green E. Join right and left leaf sections as shown (Diagram 3). Add light green Bs. Join flower section to leaf section to complete block (you may find it easier to sew the seam by hand).

Repeat to make another poppy corner block.

2. Piece the iris blocks. Join two aqua Fs to lower edges of one lavender G (Diagram 4). Join blue H to end of one aqua C as shown. Join H/C unit to edge of a white I. Make mirror-image H/C/I unit. Join H/C/I units to edges of F/G unit as shown.

Join a white J to each short edge of one dark green F. Join J/F unit to F/F edge of pieced flower. Join white K to bottom edge to complete block .

Repeat to make three more iris blocks.

3. Piece the rosebud blocks. Join one blue and one light blue V (Diagram 5). Join one lavender M to one purple M. Repeat to make another M/M unit. Join one M/M unit to the V/V unit as shown. Join remaining M/M unit to a light blue L. Stitch white Vs to edges of M/M units. Join the two halves of the rosebud as shown.

Join one white N to each upper corner of block (Diagram 6). (Stitch carefully from outside edge to inside corner of N, clip seam allowance of N at corner as shown on template, and continue stitching to end of seam.) Join white K to bottom edge to complete block. Repeat to make three more rosebud blocks.

4. Piece the tulip corner blocks. Join one light green A to one lavender C. Repeat to make a mirror-image A/C unit. Join a light green A to a dark green O as shown (Diagram 7). Join a light green P to a dark green O. Join a light green Q to another dark green O.

Lay out strips for tulip block as shown. Join rows on left half of block, then rows on right half. Join left half to right along long edge. Join light green T to block by hand.

Repeat to make another tulip corner block.

5. Piece the quilt top. Center and join 1½″-wide blue strips to all four edges of the 8½″ white center square. Miter the corners.

Join four blocks for top row as shown (Layout and Quilting Schematic). Join four blocks for bottom row, as shown. Join two blocks for each side.

Join side blocks to sides of blue/white center piece. Join top and bottom rows to top and bottom edges.

6. Add the border. Center and join 1¼″-wide white strips to all four edges of pieced blocks. Miter the corners.

Join one blue Y, one aqua X and one light blue Y as shown (Diagram 8). Repeat to make 17 more Y/X/Y units and 18 mirror-image units.

Join light blue Ys to adjacent sides of an aqua X (Diagram 8). Repeat to make three more X/Y triangles.

Join one blue X, one aqua X, and one light blue U as shown. Repeat to make three more X/U corner strips. Join two X/Y triangles to a X/U corner strip, to make a triangle corner unit. Repeat to make one more.

Join remaining Y/X/Y units to make two strips and two mirror-image strips of nine units each. Join a nine-unit Y/X/Y strip and a mirror image strip to each side of a triangle corner unit as shown. Repeat to make another strip/corner unit.

Join free ends of Y/X/Y strips to remaining X/U corner strips as shown (Diagram 9) to complete the border.

Join border to quilt, clipping blue Xs to allow you to turn the corners.

7. Mark the stems of flowers. Mark stems of flowers on quilt blocks as shown (Layout and Quilting Schematic). Embroider with outline stitch, using three strands of floss.

Quilting

1. Mark the quilting design. Trace Quilting Pattern for Center on the white center square. (Note that pattern is ¼ of design.) Match center dot on pattern with center of square and mark pattern in upper right corner of square. Repeat to mark remaining corners.

2. Stack the layers. Stack the backing (right side down), the batting, and the quilt top. Baste securely though all layers.

3. Quilt. Quilt on all marked lines with white thread. Also quilt in-the-ditch of each seam (except in border) and as close as possible to embroidered stems. Outline-quilt ¼″ inside each piece in border.

Finishing

1. Bind the edges. Join the blue bias strips to make a continuous length and use to bind edges of quilt.

Summer Flower Pillow

Materials (for one)

One completed 5½″-square pieced flower block (see instructions for quilt)
One 10″-square pillow covered in complementary fabric
¼ yard of contrasting fabric for block border and backing; matching thread
One 7″-square of polyester fleece

Pillow Assembly
Note: All seam allowances are ¼″.

1. Complete the pieced block. From contrasting fabric, cut one 8″ square for backing and four (1¾″ x 8″) pieces for border.

Mark centers of each edge of pieced block and center of one long edge of each border piece. Match center of one border piece to one edge of block. Join edges to within ¼″ of corner. Repeat to join remaining border pieces to remaining edges. Miter the corners.

Pin fleece to wrong side of pieced block. Join backing to pieced block with right sides together, securing fleece and leaving a small opening for turning. Clip corners. Turn. Slipstitch the opening closed.

2. Add block to pillow. Place the block diagonally on pillow. Tack corners of block to secure it to pillow side seams.

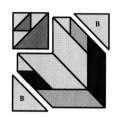

Diagram 3

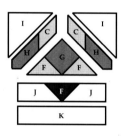

Diagram 4

Layout and Quilting Schematic
Note: Dotted lines indicate quilting.

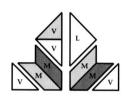

Diagram 5

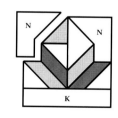

Diagram 6

Diagram 1

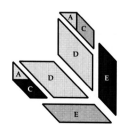

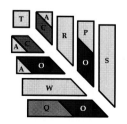

Diagram 2

Diagram 7

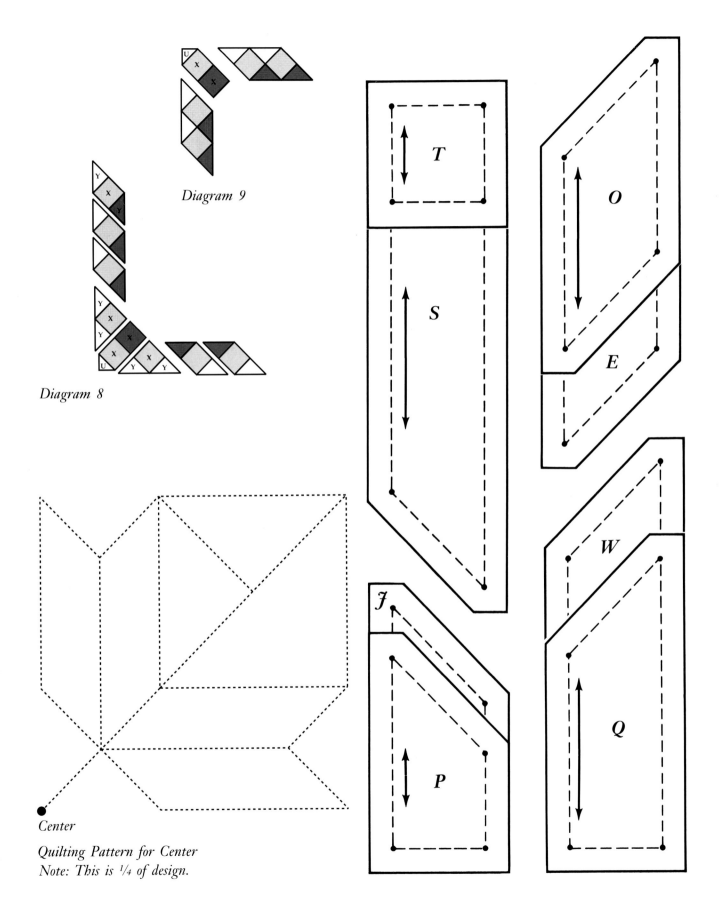

Diagram 9

Diagram 8

Center

Quilting Pattern for Center
Note: This is ¼ of design.

T

S

O

E

J

P

W

Q

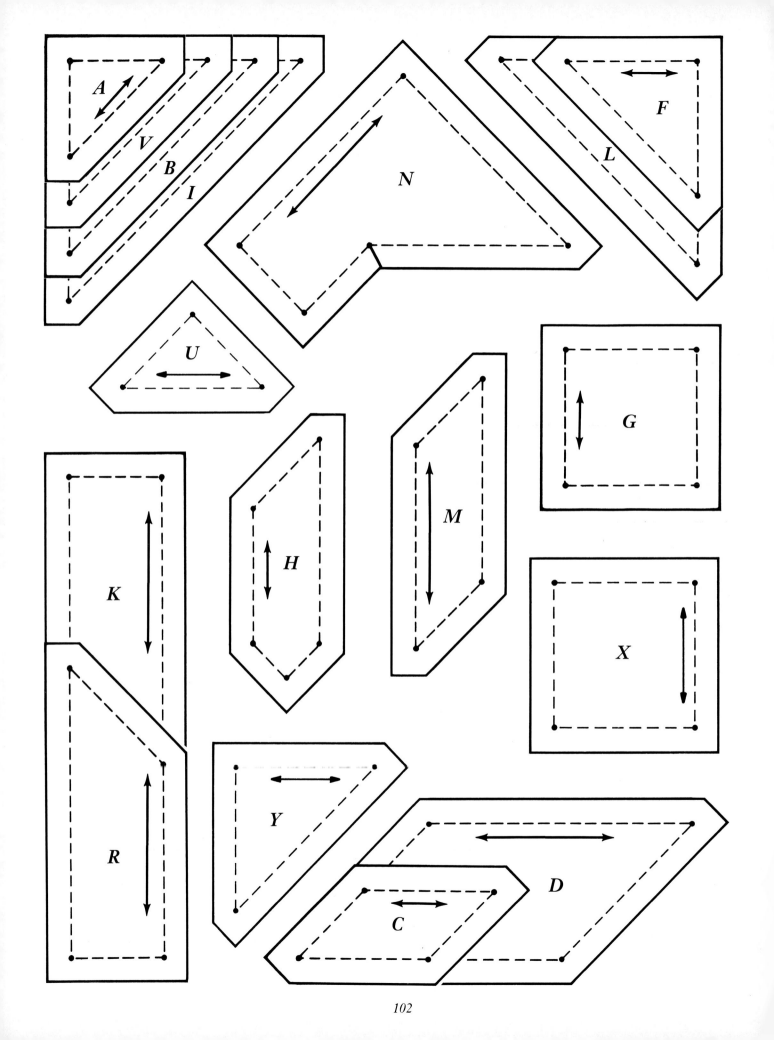

Harvest

Smooth, fat buttons stand in for kernels of corn and watermelon seeds on a whimsical quilt that fairly begs to be touched. Use it as a memorable centerpiece for special family dinners, or enjoy it every day as a kitchen hanging.

Quilt Top Assembly

Note: All seam allowances are ¼".

1. Piece the top. Join one rose 3" square to one green 3" square. Repeat to make nine more rose/green rectangles. Join two rectangles, alternating colors, to make

a checkerboard. Repeat to make 4 more checkerboard blocks. Join checkerboard blocks to white blocks as shown (Diagram 1), to make 3 rows. Join rows as shown to complete piecing of quilt top.

Mark quilting patterns for food designs on white blocks; see Quilting Schematic for placement. Appliqué corn husk (A), pea pod (B), and grape leaf (C). Pin watermelon center (D) onto block. Appliqué top edge only; then appliqué watermelon rind (E).

Quilting

1. Mark the quilting design. In addition to quilting patterns for corn, peas, and grapes, mark diagonal lines on white squares as shown (Quilting Schematic). Mark additional diagonal lines in the checkerboard blocks to make a grid pattern.

2. Stack the layers. Stack the quilt backing (right side down), fleece, and quilt top. Baste securely through all layers.

3. Quilt. Use green thread to quilt on all marked lines. In addition, quilt lines as shown to outline watermelon, and to indicate inner leaves of corn husk and fold line of pea pod. Also quilt on each white block, as close as possible to the inside edge of the seam line. Quilt on watermelon center, next to the rind, with red thread.

Trim edges of backing and fleece to match top of quilt.

Finishing

1. Bind the edges. Join 1¾" x 15½" red polished cotton strips to top and bottom edges of quilt. Fold excess fabric to wrong side of quilt, turn under seam allowances, and slipstitch folded edge to backing. Sew remaining strips to right and left edges of quilt. Turn under seam allowances at ends of strips. Fold excess fabric to wrong side, turn under seam allowance on long edge, and slipstitch folded edge to backing. Whipstitch ends closed to complete binding.

2. Attach the buttons. Sew buttons to quilt top (see photo for placement).

Layout Schematic

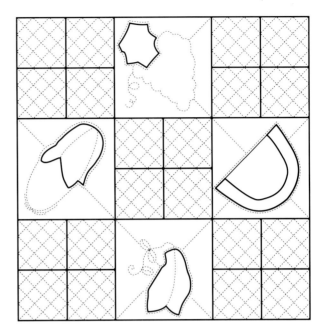

Quilting Schematic

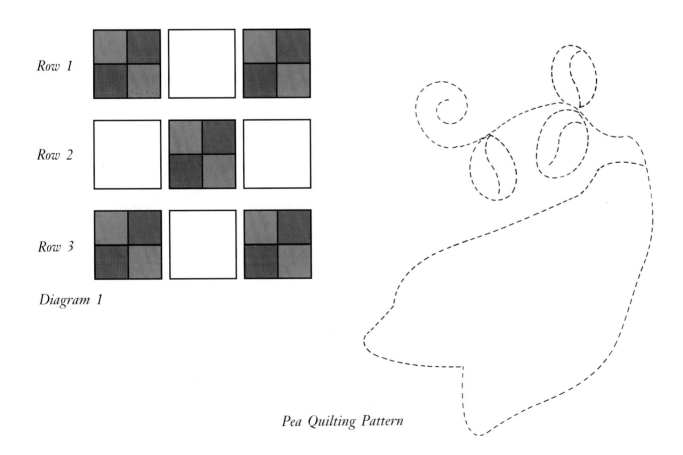

Row 1

Row 2

Row 3

Diagram 1

Pea Quilting Pattern

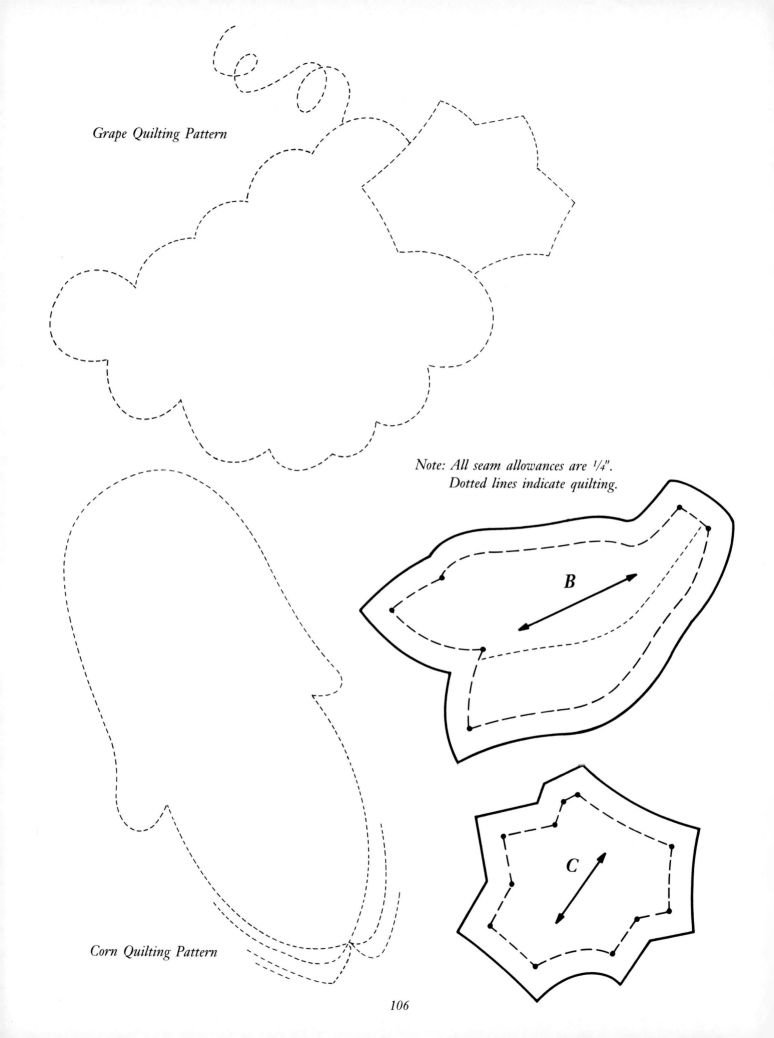

Grape Quilting Pattern

Note: All seam allowances are ¼".
Dotted lines indicate quilting.

B

C

Corn Quilting Pattern

106

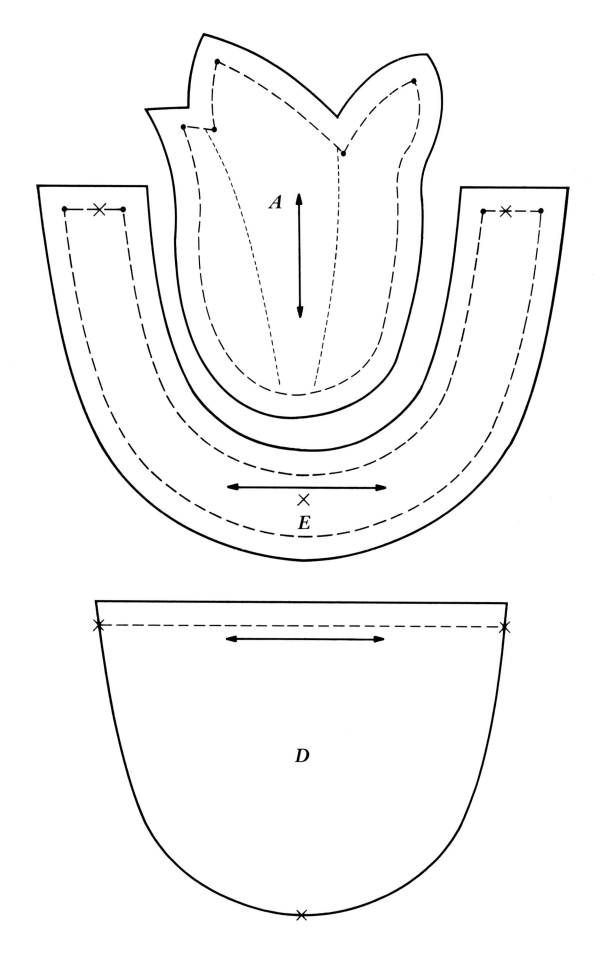

A

E

D

In Full Bloom

Inspired by the radiant energy of high summer, this quilt displays a clever combination of precision piecing and simple appliqué. Each appliquéd blossom is actually a circle, pieced from colorful petal shapes and triangles of background fabric.

Finished size of quilt: *40½" x 40½"*

Materials

Burgundy: ¼ yard
  Pieces to cut: 48 (template E), 3 (template J), 12 (template A)

Burgundy print: ½ yard
  Pieces to cut: 84 (template E), 9 (template J), 1 (template D)

Pink/burgundy print: ⅜ yard
  Pieces to cut: 84 (template E), 12 (template B) 6 (template J)

Pink/cream print: ¼ yard
  Pieces to cut: 36 (template E), 5 (template J)

Rust: ¼ yard
  Pieces to cut: 36 (template E), 1 (template J)

Dk. green: 1⅝ yards
  Pieces to cut: 32 (template G), 32 (template H), 4 (template I), 4½ yards of ⅞"-wide bias strips for stems, 5 yards of 2"-wide bias strips for binding

Lt. green: ⅛ yard
  Pieces to cut: 17 (template G)

Small green print: ⅛ yard
  Pieces to cut: 18 (template G)

Large green print: ⅛ yard
  Pieces to cut: 29 (template G)

Cream/white print: 3½ yards
  Pieces to cut: 12 (template C), 288 (template F), 36 (template H), 1 (36½" square) for top, 1 (42½" square) for backing

Polyester fleece: 1¼ yards
  Pieces to cut: 1 (40½" square)

Cream thread for quilting
Compass for marking circles

Quilt Top Assembly

Note: All seam allowances are ¼". After piecing, it may be necessary to trim some seam allowances to ⅛". As a general rule, if seam allowances touch each other on the back when the block is pressed, they should be trimmed.

1. Make the center flower. Join one burgundy A to one pink/burgundy print B. Repeat to make 11 more A/B units. Add a cream/white print C to the right edge of each A/B unit (Diagram 1). Join A/B/C units to make a circle (Diagram 2). Join burgundy print D to center of flower. Set aside.

2. Make the 24 small blossom blocks. Join an E to a cream/white print F. Repeat to make eleven more E/F units. Join units to make a circle (Diagram 3). Join a J to center of circle. Repeat to make 23 more small blossom blocks. Set aside.

3. Mark the top. Fold the 36½" square of cream/white fabric in half, horizontally and then vertically. Lightly mark the fold lines to divide quilt top into quarters.

Mark diagonal lines from corner to corner of quilt (Diagram 4). Use a compass to center and draw a 6"-diameter circle in the center of the quilt.

Make a mark 10" out from the center of the quilt on each horizontal, vertical, and diagonal line (As on Diagram 4). Center and draw a 4"-diameter circle on each A.

Make marks 15½" out from center of quilt on horizontal and vertical lines. Center and draw a 4"-diameter circle on each of these marks. Divide each of these circles into quarters, showing the divisions on outside of circle with dots (Diagram 4). Mark arc lines on quilt as shown by placing point of compass on center of each A and placing point of pencil on the corresponding Bs.

Mark a 7¾" square in each corner of the quilt as shown (Diagram 4). Make a mark on each diagonal line of the quilt, 4¾" from the outside corner. Center a 4" circle on each mark. Make a mark on each inside edge of the 7¾" square, 2¼" in from outside edge of quilt. Center a 4" circle on each of these marks.

4. Appliqué the stems and leaves. Use the circles, straight lines, and arc lines to position flowers and stems. Cut eight (3½") pieces of ⅞" dark green bias strip. Center and appliqué strips over marked lines between large center flower and inner circle of small blossoms (Layout Schematic).

Cut eight (10½") pieces of ⅞" dark green bias strip. Center and appliqué over arc lines.

Cut four (8") and eight (3½") lengths of ⅞" dark green bias strip to make stems for flowers in corners of quilt. Appliqué side stems first, centering 3½" strips over lines; then appliqué 8" center stems. Appliqué leaves (G) as shown, noting that about every third leaf is dark green.

5. Appliqué the flowers. Turn under seam allowance on center flower and small blossoms and appliqué them to quilt top in positions shown (Layout Schematic), placing colors as desired. (Note: There will be two layers of fabric on the quilt top wherever there are appliqués. To make quilting easier, trim backing fabric from behind appliqués, leaving ¼" of seam allowance.)

6. Add the border. Join nine cream/white Hs with eight dark green Hs, alternating colors. Repeat to make three more border strips. Join strips to sides of quilt top. Join one dark green I to each corner of border.

Quilting

1. Mark the quilting design. Use the quilting patterns to mark quilting lines in the centers of flowers, in green H blocks of border, and in center of quilt as shown (Quilting Schematic). Mark quilting lines ¼" inside seams on all white blocks. Also mark quilting lines ¼" outside appliquéd stems and leaves and inside leaves, as shown, and outside flower petals. Mark ½" diamond grid to fill remaining space in cream/white area of border and background as indicated in Quilting Schematic.

2. Stack the layers. Stack the quilt backing (right side down), fleece, and top. Baste securely through all layers.

3. Quilt. Quilt on all marked lines with cream thread. Also quilt in-the-ditch around the outside edge of the center flower and each small blossom. Trim edges of backing and fleece to match quilt top.

Finishing

1. Bind the edges. Join the 2" dark green bias strips to make a continuous length and use it to bind the edges.

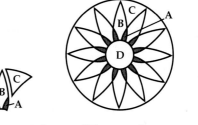

Diagram 1   *Diagram 2*   *Diagram 3*

Layout Schematic

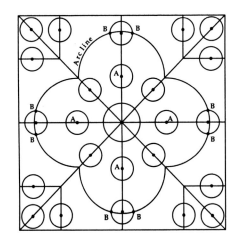

Diagram 4: Marking the Quilt Top

Flower Center Quilting Pattern

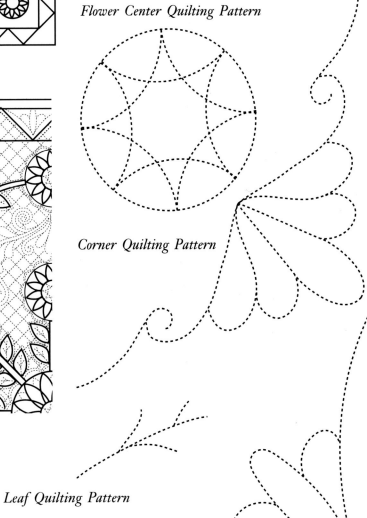

Corner Quilting Pattern

Quilting Schematic
Note: Dotted lines indicate quilting.
This is ¼ of design.

Leaf Quilting Pattern

Border Quilting Pattern

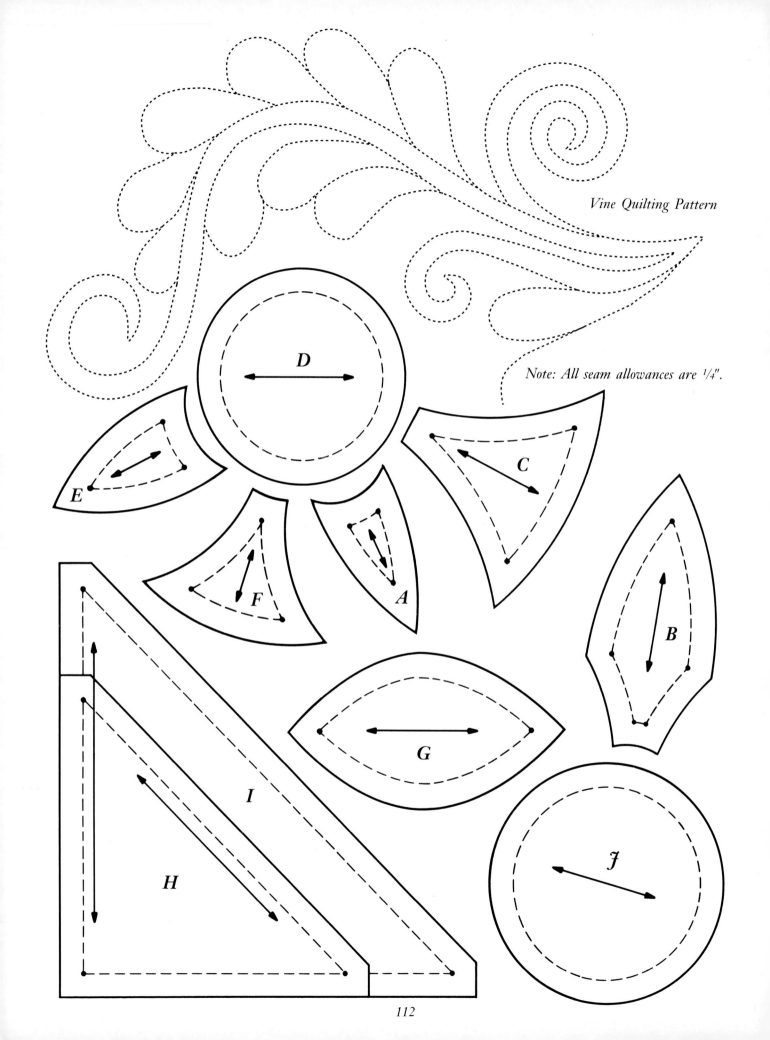

Vine Quilting Pattern

Note: All seam allowances are ¼".

D

E

C

F

A

B

H

I

G

J

112

Shades of Twilight

*Like a landscape viewed in the hour between twilight and darkness, this
quilt delights the eye with a gradual shading of color
from palest tints to deepest shades. The hand-dyed muslins that
were used to piece it can be ordered by mail.*

Quilt Top Assembly

Note: All seam allowances are ¼". After stitching, it may be necessary to trim some to ⅛". As a general rule, if the pieces are so small that seam allowances touch each other on the back after stitching, they should be trimmed to ⅛".

1. Sort the fabrics. For each color in this quilt (green, blue, brown, gray, and purple), you will have 6 shades, ranging from very light to very dark. Sort the fabrics into 6 piles that correspond to the 6 shades. Place the lightest green, the lightest brown, etc., in the first pile. Place the next lightest fabrics in the 2nd pile and so on, ending with the darkest fabrics in the 6th pile.

Use the fabrics from the first pile to make blocks 1 and 2. (Since the fabrics are hand-dyed, there will be slight variations of color within each piece of fabric. For greater variety, cut the pieces for block 1 from the lighter areas of the appropriate fabrics and pieces for block 2 from the darker areas.) Use fabrics from pile 2 for blocks 3 and 4, pile 3 for blocks 5 and 6, pile 4 for blocks 7 and 8, pile 5 for blocks 9 and 10, and pile 6 for blocks 11 and 12.

2. Make the top halves of blocks 1, 7, and 11.

Note: Make top halves of all blocks first, using templates to cut pattern pieces.

Cut one 2½" x 2¾" piece from the lightest purple fabric and cut another from the lightest green fabric. Join along long edge. Place template A over the strip as shown (Diagram 1) and cut out a two-color triangle. Reposition template A on strip and cut out another triangle, making it a mirror-image of the first A (Diagram 3).

Join and cut additional strips to make 2 mirror-image purple/brown triangles and 2 mirror-image green/blue triangles.

To make the two-color squares, cut a 4½" x 1¼" piece from light brown fabric and one from gray. Join along long edge. Position template B on strip as shown (Diagram 2) and cut out a two-color square. Repeat once. Cut two Cs, one G, and three Ds, referring to Diagram 4, block 1, for colors. Join pieces to make four strips as shown (Diagram 3). Join strips to complete top half of block 1.

To make top halves of blocks 7 and 11, repeat, using colors indicated for these blocks (Diagram 4).

3. Make the top halves of blocks 2, 3, and 8. To make top half of block 2, cut out and join 2 purple Cs along short edge. Repeat to make a blue C/C triangle and a brown C/C triangle.

Cut 2 green Es, 2 gray Ds, 2 brown Ds, and one purple G. Join in rows as indicated (Diagram 4), to complete block 2.

Repeat, using colors indicated in Diagram 4, to make top halves for blocks 3 and 8.

4. Make the top halves of blocks 4, 6, 10, and 12. To make top half of block 4, cut and join pieces, as indicated (Diagram 4). Repeat to make top halves for blocks 6, 10, 12.

5. Make the top halves of remaining blocks. Cut and join fabrics as indicated (Diagram 4) to complete top halves for blocks 5 and 9.

6. Make the bottom halves of blocks 1, 4, 5, 6, 7, and 11. Note: Make bottom halves of blocks using fabric strips cut to size without templates. For block 1, using fabrics from pile 1, cut a $1\frac{3}{8}$" x $1\frac{3}{8}$" piece of green fabric , a $1\frac{3}{8}$" x $2\frac{1}{4}$" piece of blue, a $1\frac{3}{8}$" x $3\frac{1}{8}$" piece of gray, and a $1\frac{3}{8}$" x 4" piece of brown. Match long edges of strips and join (Diagram 5).

Join strips for blocks 4, 5, 6, 7, and 11 as above, referring to Diagram 4 for colors and placement.

Place template F over each pieced triangle, matching right angles. Trim off excess fabric on long edge of triangle to match template F.

7. Make the bottom halves of blocks 2, 9, and 12. Cut strips for piecing bottom half of block 2 as follows: 1 ($1\frac{1}{8}$" x $1\frac{1}{8}$") brown, 1 ($1\frac{1}{8}$" x $1\frac{3}{4}$") gray, 1 ($1\frac{1}{8}$" x $2\frac{3}{8}$") blue, 1 ($1\frac{1}{8}$" x 3") green, 1 ($1\frac{1}{8}$" x 3") brown, 1 ($1\frac{1}{8}$" x $2\frac{3}{8}$") gray, 1 ($1\frac{1}{8}$" x $1\frac{3}{4}$") blue, and 1 ($1\frac{1}{8}$" x $1\frac{1}{8}$") green. Match long edges of strips and join as shown in Diagram 6, referring to Diagram 4 for color and placement. Repeat to make bottom halves of blocks 9 and 12.

Place template F over each pieced triangle, matching long edge of F to long edge of triangle. Trim short edges of triangles to match F.

8. Make the bottom halves of blocks 3, 8, and 10. To make block 3, cut strips as follows: 1 ($1\frac{1}{8}$" x $1\frac{5}{8}$") brown, 1 ($1\frac{1}{8}$" x $2\frac{7}{8}$") gray, 1 ($1\frac{1}{8}$" x $4\frac{1}{4}$") blue, and 1 ($1\frac{1}{8}$" x $5\frac{1}{2}$") green. Match edges and join as shown in Diagram 7. Repeat to make bottom halves of blocks 8 and 10, referring to Diagram 4 for colors.

Place template F over pieced triangle, matching long edge of F to long edge of triangle. Trim short edges of

pieced triangle to match F.

Repeat, referring to Diagram 4 for colors, to cut and join strips for triangles 8 and 10. Trim edges, using template F as a guide.

9. Complete the blocks. Join top halves to bottom halves along long edges as shown (Diagram 4) to complete blocks.

10. Add the sashing. To assemble row 1, join blocks 4, 2, and 1 with 4 ($1\frac{3}{8}$" x 4") light purple strips. Join rows 2-4 in same way.

Join 4 ($1\frac{3}{8}$" x $1\frac{3}{8}$") brown squares with 3 ($1\frac{3}{8}$" x 4") light purple strips between, to make a row of sashing (Layout Schematic). Repeat to make 4 more rows.

Alternate rows of sashing with rows of blocks, beginning and ending with sashing. Join to complete top.

11. Make the corded piping. To make corded piping, cut six ($1\frac{1}{4}$" x 12") bias strips from four different purple fabrics, repeating the middle two shades. Join strips in desired order to make a continuous length. Cover the cording with the bias strip to make the piping.

Stitch piping to right side of quilt top.

Quilting

1. Stack the layers. Stack the backing (right side down), flannel, and quilt top. Baste securely through all layers.

2. Quilt. Quilt with white thread on every seam line. Quilt additional areas as desired in Blocks 4, 5, 6, 9, 10, and 12. Trim flannel to match top.

Finishing

1. Finish the edges. Fold seam allowances of the piping to the inside. Trim seam allowance of backing to $\frac{1}{4}$". Quilt along the folded outside edge of the sashing. Fold the backing to the inside and slipstitch to the piping.

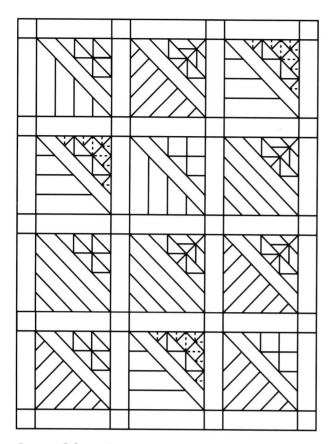

Layout Schematic

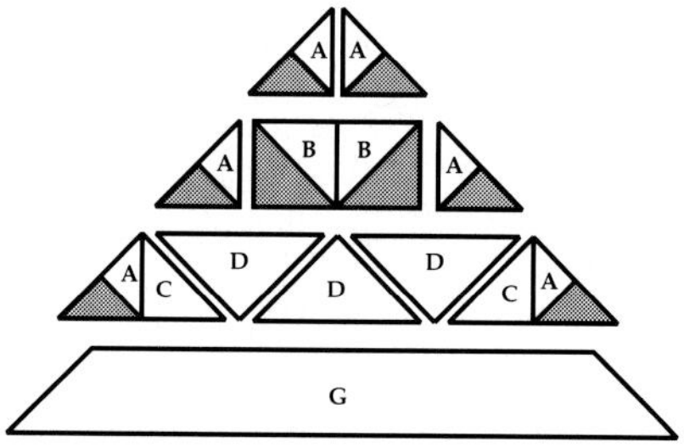

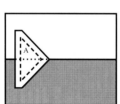

Diagram 1

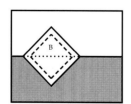

Diagram 2

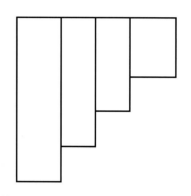

Diagram 3

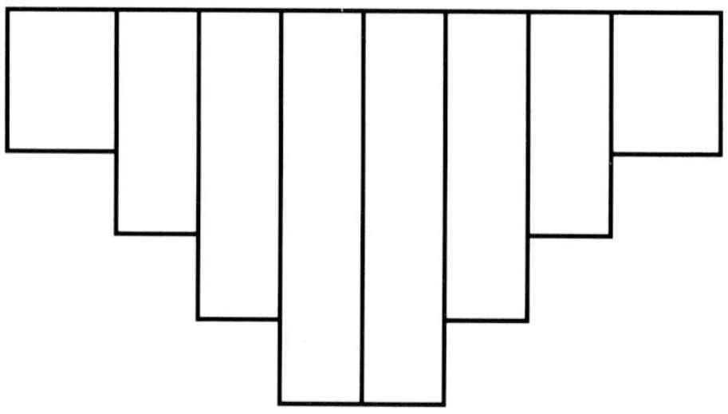

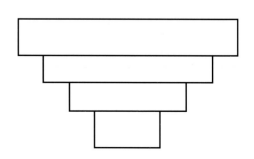

Diagram 5

Diagram 6

Diagram 7

Diagram 4: Piecing the Blocks   Color Code: bl—blue
                                    p—purple   gr—green
                                    gy—gray   br—brown

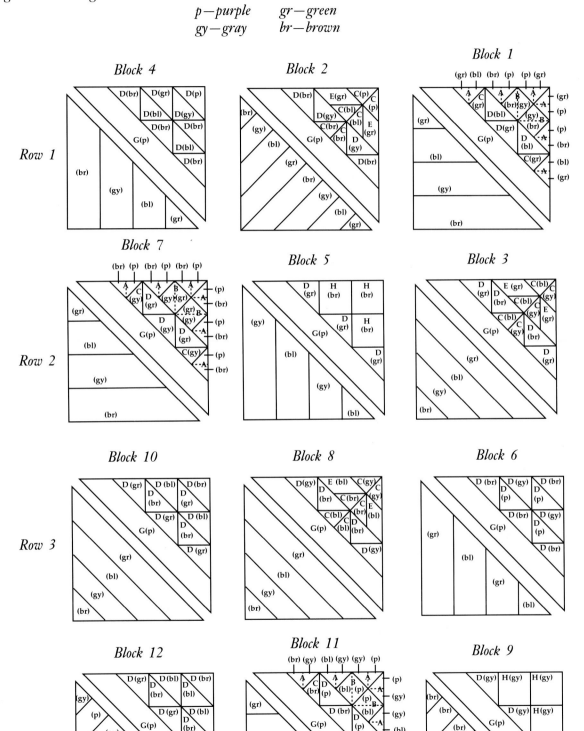

117

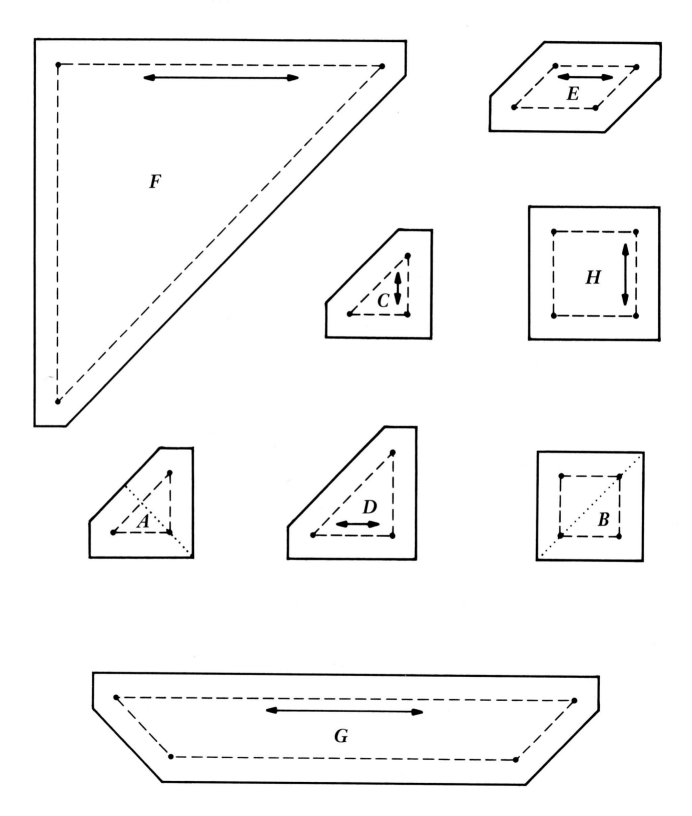

Cow in the Clover

One block, one border, and a charming country cow that's fun to appliqué. This is a quilt you can cut, stitch, and quilt in a weekend, making it just right for quick gifts or to give a lift to your decorating.

Finished size of quilt: 16½″ x 16½″

Materials

Unbleached muslin: ⅝ yard
  Pieces to cut: 1 (18½″ square) for backing, 1 (10″ x 7″) for cow appliqué

Green: scraps
  Pieces to cut: 2 (template A)

Green print: scraps
  Pieces to cut: 2 (template A)

Pink: ⅛ yard
  Pieces to cut: 4 (2½″ x 10″)

Cream/pink print: scraps
  Pieces to cut: 4 (template B)

Blue-green: ¼ yard
  Pieces to cut: 4 (1½″ x 16½″) for border

Polyester fleece: ½ yard
  Pieces to cut: 1 (16½″ square)

Green thread for quilting
Fabric paints: gold, pink, black
Paintbrush
Black permanent fine-point pen

Quilt Top Assembly

Note: All seam allowances are ¼″.

1. Piece the background. Join one green A to one green print A. Repeat to make second A/A triangle. Join the A/A triangles to make the center square, with the print pieces at top and bottom (Diagram 1).

2. Add the border. Join pink strips to left and right edges of center square. Join cream/pink Bs to ends of one remaining pink strip. Repeat for second strip. Join pieced strips to top and bottom of center square (Diagram 2).

Join blue-green strips to left and right edges of border. Trim excess. Join remaining blue-green strips to top and bottom borders (Layout Schematic).

3. Appliqué the cow. Use template C to trace the cow pattern onto the muslin. Paint each area as shown (see pattern and photo). Outline the cow with the black pen. Cut out cow. Center the cow on the pieced quilt top. Appliqué it to top, turning edge under just outside the pen line.

Quilting

1. Mark the quilt design. Mark echo-quilting lines ¼″ apart, inside all A triangles, following seam lines along outside edges and gradually changing to follow outline of cow along inside edges. Mark echo-quilting lines ¼″ apart on each border and corner piece.

2. Stack the layers. Stack the quilt backing (right side down), fleece, and quilt top. Baste securely through all layers.

3. Quilt. Quilt all lines with green thread. Trim edges of backing to match quilt top.

Layout Schematic

Finishing

1. Frame. Have a professional framer cover the mat with a coordinating print fabric. Frame the quilt with a plain ⅝″-wide wooden frame painted to coordinate with fabric.

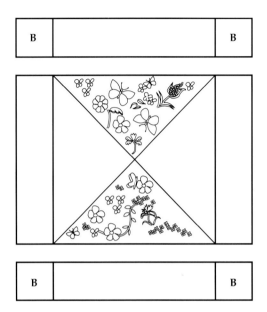

Diagram 2: Assembling Quilt Center

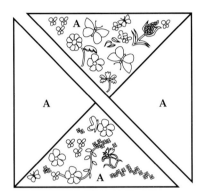

Diagram 1

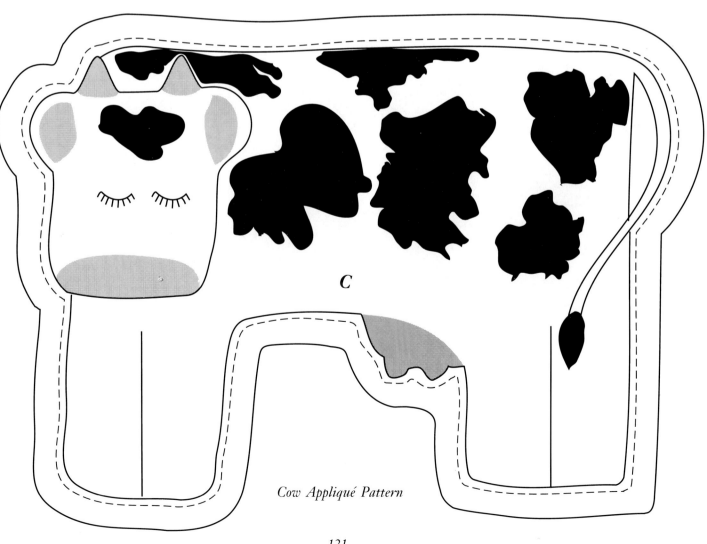

Cow Appliqué Pattern

Note: All seam allowances are ¹/₄".

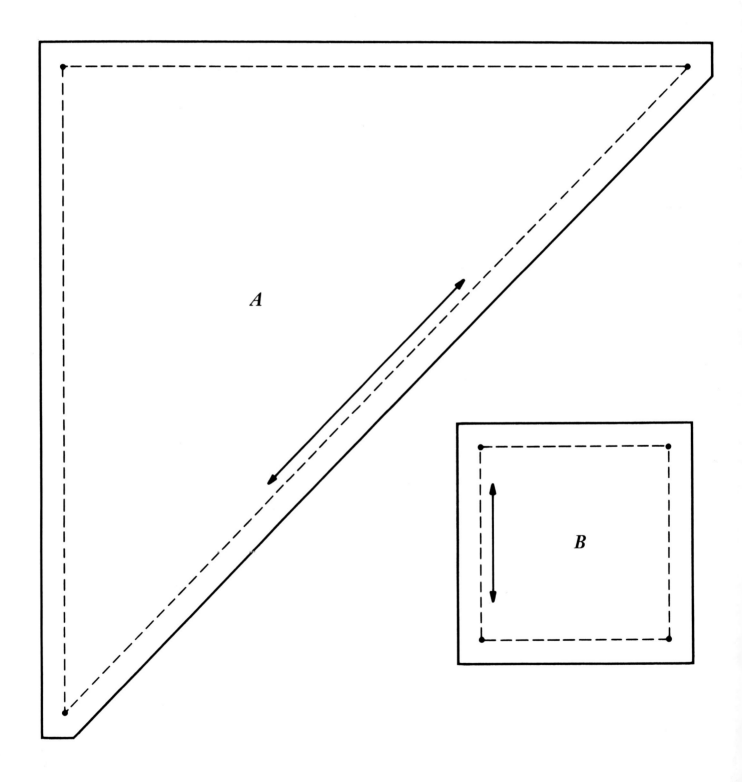

Grandmother's Quilt

Here's a gift any grandmother will love—a hand-stitched quilt with an appliquéd heart for each of her grandchildren. Embroider one grandchild's name and date of birth on each heart square and add an extra heart or two for names of grandchildren yet to come.

Quilt Top Assembly

Note: All seam allowances are ¼".

1. Prepare the heart/squares section. Piece the muslin background for the heart appliqués as shown (Diagram 1).

Trim the ¼" seam allowance from template B to make a finished-size template. Trace heart outline onto the muslin squares, with hearts centered on squares as shown (Layout Schematic). Using heart outline as a guide, appliqué hearts to squares. Mark placement for dates and signatures on heart squares with a pencil. Sign with permanent pen. Add personal note or poem in empty block (see photo).

2. Appliqué the figures. Fold muslin strip in half to find center line. Center one D on this line and appliqué to muslin strip. Center Es over seam lines at ends of strip as shown (Diagram 2). Appliqué to strip. (Trim excess fabric from outer edges of Es after appliquéing.) Place remaining Ds and Es as shown, adjusting positions so that hands just touch. Appliqué figures to complete strip.

3. Make the small heart band. Alternate 1¼" x 2" brown print strips with muslin Cs to form a band (Diagram 3). Join 23¾" brown print strips to upper and lower edges. Center and trace a small heart (template F) in center of each muslin C, using permanent pen (see photo).

Match edges and join the small heart band between the top section and the bottom section.

4. Add the border. Center and stitch one 4½" x 33¾" brown print border strip to bottom edge of quilt top. Center and stitch remaining three border pieces to sides and top. Miter the corners.

Quilting

1. Mark the quilting design. Mark horizontal quilting lines that extend the top and bottom seam lines of the small heart band out into the print border (Quilting Schematic). Transfer quilting patterns to the large appliquéd hearts, repeating them as desired.

Mark extensions of seam lines joining triangles and squares in the heart/squares section out onto the brown print borders. Then draw a line halfway between each of these extensions to make a diamond pattern in the border. Duplicate the diamond pattern in the bottom border. Outline-quilt diamonds as shown.

2. Stack the layers. Stack the backing (right side down), fleece, and quilt top. Baste securely through all layers.

3. Quilt. Quilt lines marked in hearts with matching thread. Using light brown thread, quilt on all marked lines and in-the-ditch of seams on muslin, around each heart, around each figure, and on all lines in the border. Trim backing and fleece to match quilt top.

Finishing

1. Bind the edges. Join strips of brown print bias fabric to make a continuous length and use it to bind edges of quilt.

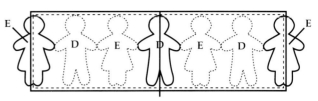

Center line

Diagram 2: Appliquéing Figures to Muslin Strip

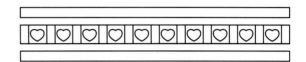

Diagram 3: Assembling Small Heart Band

Layout Schematic

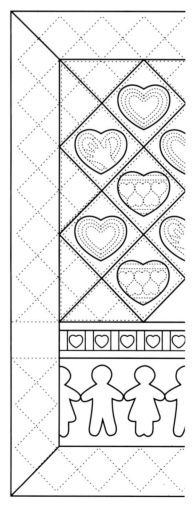

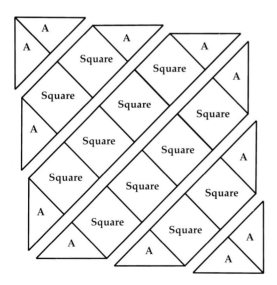

Diagram 1: Piecing Background for Hearts

Quilting Schematic
Note: Dotted lines indicate quilting.

Quilting Pattern #1

Quilting Pattern #2

Quilting Pattern #3

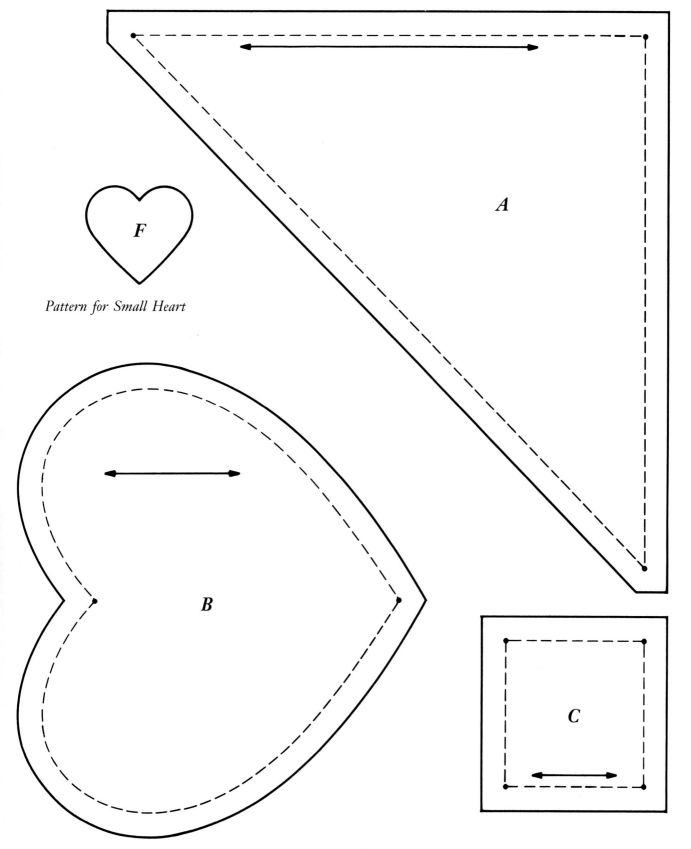

F

Pattern for Small Heart

A

B

C

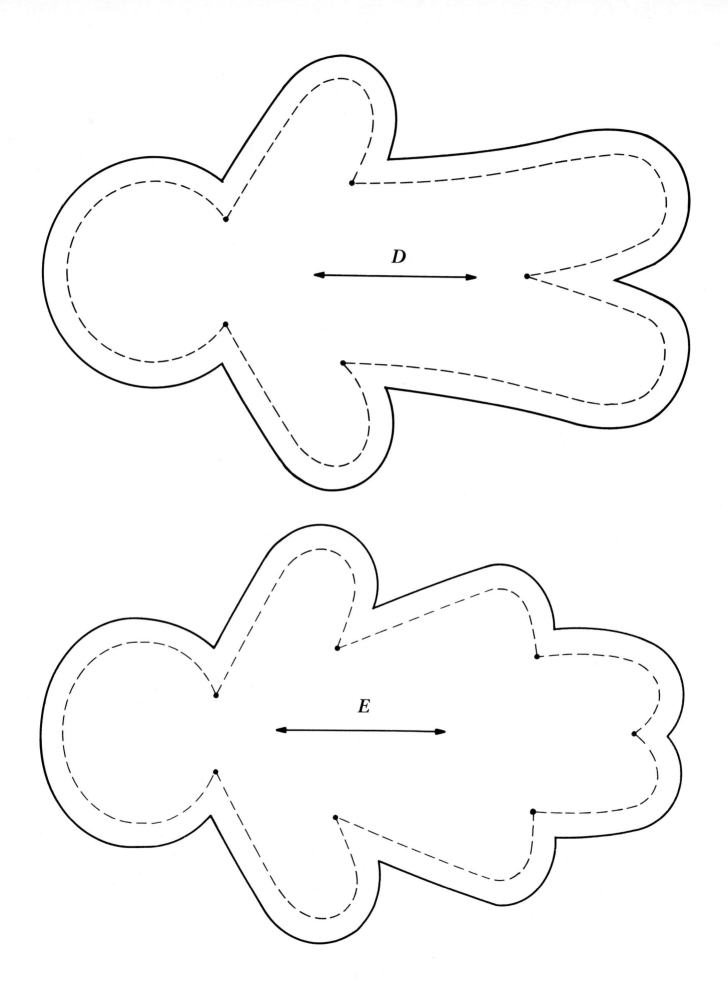

Warmhearted Snowflake

*Bright Pennsylvania German appliqué centers a collection of carved
folk art Santas. In this quilt, the airy design of
shapes cut from blue, green, and red fabric is balanced
by large areas of fine quilting.*

Finished size of quilt: *38" x 38"*

Materials

Muslin: 2¼ yards
  Pieces to cut: 1 (38" square) quilt top, 1 (40" square) for backing

Blue: ¾ yard
  Pieces to cut: 48 (template A), 40 (template B), 4½ yards of 1¼"-wide bias strips for corded piping

Red: ¼ yard
  Pieces to cut: 57 (template B), 24 (template C)

Green: ¼ yard
  Pieces to cut: 164 (template D)

Polyester fleece: 1⅛ yards
  Pieces to cut: 1 (38" square)

Cream thread for quilting
Thread to match appliqué pieces
4½ yards of ¼"-wide cording

Quilt Top Assembly

Note: Appliqués have ⅛" seam allowances. All other seam allowances are ¼".

1. **Mark the top**. Mark horizontal and vertical center lines on the smaller muslin square, to divide it into quarters. Mark a dot (A) in exact center of square. Divide square diagonally by marking lines from corner to corner (Diagram 1).

   Mark a dot (B) on each diagonal line, 11½" out from the center dot. Mark a borderline 2" in from, and parallel to, each outside edge of square as shown.

   Using Appliqué and Quilting Guide for Center Snowflake as a pattern, align center circle of design with dot A at center of quilt and trace entire center design as shown, in exact center of muslin square. (Note: Pattern is ¼ of design.) Using Appliqué and Quilting Guide for Corner Snowflake, and referring to Layout Schematic for placement, align center circle on corner pattern with dot B marked on diagonal line and trace corner design in one corner as shown. Repeat to mark other corners.

   Align outside edge of Appliqué and Quilting Guide for Border with marked borderline. Trace corner section of border pattern first. For the rest of border, mark repeats (shaded area) at 3" intervals as shown.

2. **Appliqué the pieces.** Using traced design as a guide, appliqué each piece individually with matching thread, beginning with pieces at the center of the quilt and working out toward the edges.

Quilting

1. **Mark the quilting design.** Refer to Quilting Schematic to mark the remaining quilting. Divide the marked horizontal and vertical lines on the quilt into ⅝" intervals. Draw a line from each mark to center of the adjacent corner design to begin a series of radiating lines (Quilting Schematic). Extend each line to other side of corner motif to complete the pattern.

2. **Stack the layers.** Stack the quilt backing (right side down), fleece, and appliquéd top. Baste securely through all layers.

3. **Quilt.** Quilt with cream thread on all marked lines and as closely as possible to each appliqué.

Finishing

1. **Trim**. Trim ¼" from all edges of fleece. Trim quilt backing to same size as quilt top.

2. **Finish the edges.** Join the blue bias strips to make a continuous length and use it to make 4½ yards of corded piping. Trim the seam allowance of the piping to ¼". With raw edges aligned, join piping to right side of quilt top, stitching ¼" in from the edge and rounding the corners slightly. Fold raw edges of piping to the inside. Fold seam allowance of backing to inside. Slip-stitch backing to quilt top.

Layout Schematic

Quilting Schematic
Note: This is ¹/₄ of design.

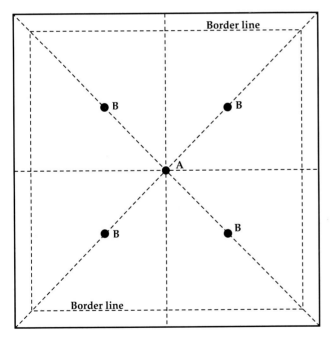

Diagram 1: Marking the Muslin Square

Note: Seam allowances on appliqués are ¹/₈". All other seam allowances are ¹/₄".

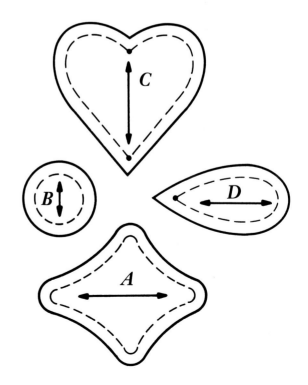

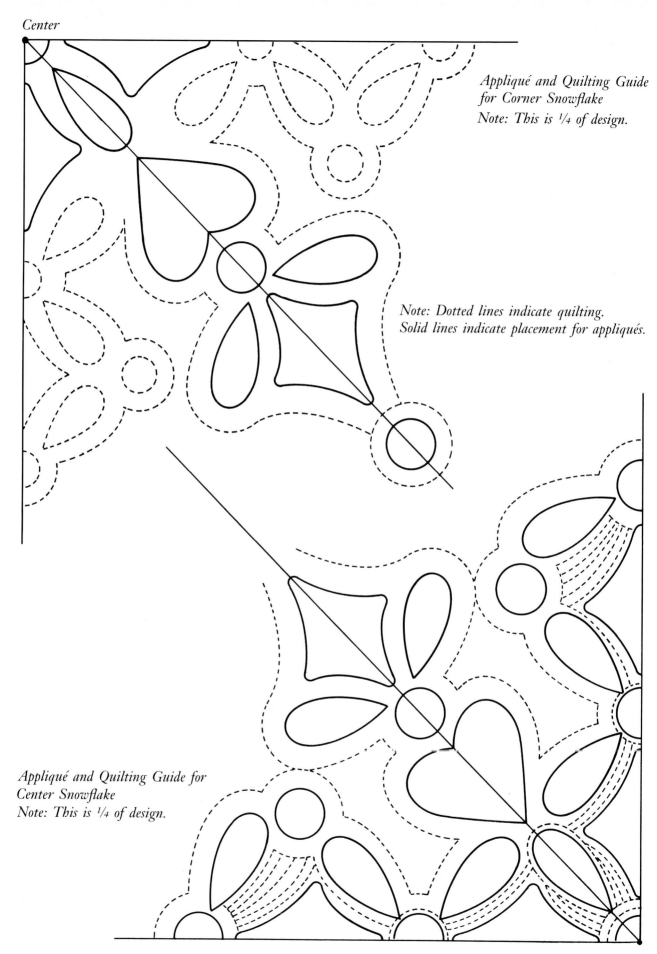

Center

*Appliqué and Quilting Guide
for Corner Snowflake
Note: This is ¼ of design.*

*Note: Dotted lines indicate quilting.
Solid lines indicate placement for appliqués.*

*Appliqué and Quilting Guide for
Center Snowflake
Note: This is ¼ of design.*

Center

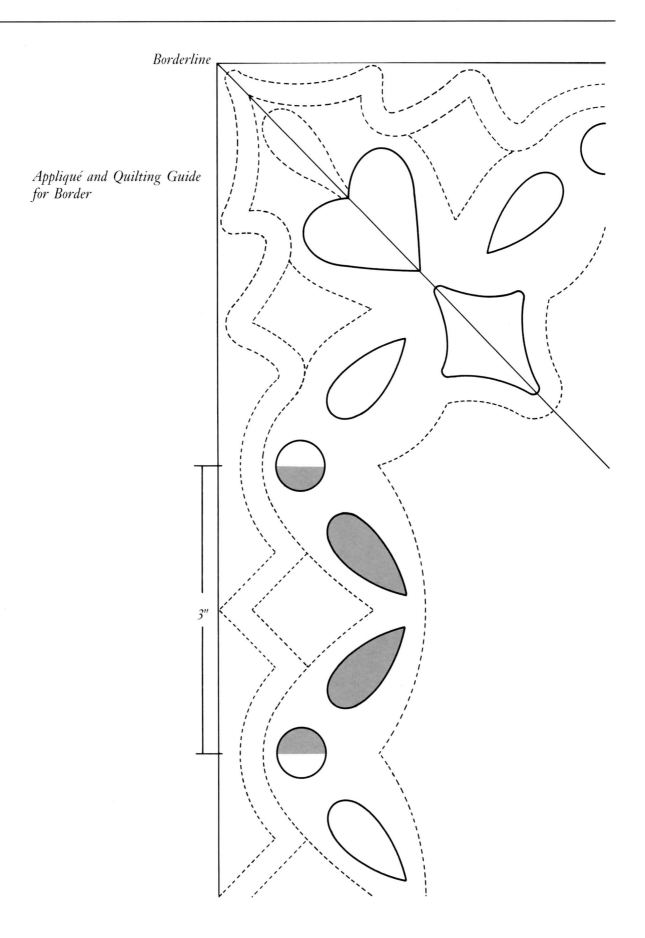

Borderline

Appliqué and Quilting Guide for Border

3″

Friendship Wreath

Now that quilts are a pleasure instead of a necessity, you no longer have to stitch a full-size bed covering to sample the fine art of hand appliqué. One block is enough for a handsome hanging, so take your time and enjoy every stitch, as you shape the curves and layer the hearts and flowers of this delicate design.

Finished size of quilt: *25½" x 25½"*

Materials

Dk. blue print: ½ yard
  Pieces to cut: 1 (15" square)

Red/white pindot: ⅜ yard
  Pieces to cut: 1 (template B), 10 (template D), 3 (template J)

Green: 4" square
  Pieces to cut: 1 (template A)

Dk. green print: 5" square
  Pieces to cut: 1 (template C)

Lt. green print: scraps
  Pieces to cut: 8 (template F)

Med. blue print: scraps
  Pieces to cut: 2 (template G1)

Lt. blue print: scraps
  Pieces to cut: 2 (template G2)

Pale yellow print: scraps
  Pieces to cut: 5 (template M), 1 (template J)

Gold: scraps
  Pieces to cut: 2 (template H)

Pink: scraps
  Pieces to cut: 2 (template L)

Rust: scraps
  Pieces to cut: 1 (template K)

Cream: ⅛ yard
  Pieces to cut: 2 (template K), 1 (template H), 4 (¾" x 16") for sashing

Blue/navy pindot: 9" square
  Pieces to cut: 1 (template E)

Green print: ¾ yard
  Pieces to cut: 5 (1½" x 20") for checkerboard corner squares, 3 yards of 1½"-wide bias strips for binding

Navy print: ¾ yard
  Pieces to cut: 1 (27½" square) for backing, 4 (5½" x 15½"), 5 (1½" x 20") for checkerboard corner squares, 13 (template I), 1 (template L)

Polyester fleece: ¾ yard
  Pieces to cut: 1 (25½" square)

Yellow thread for quilting

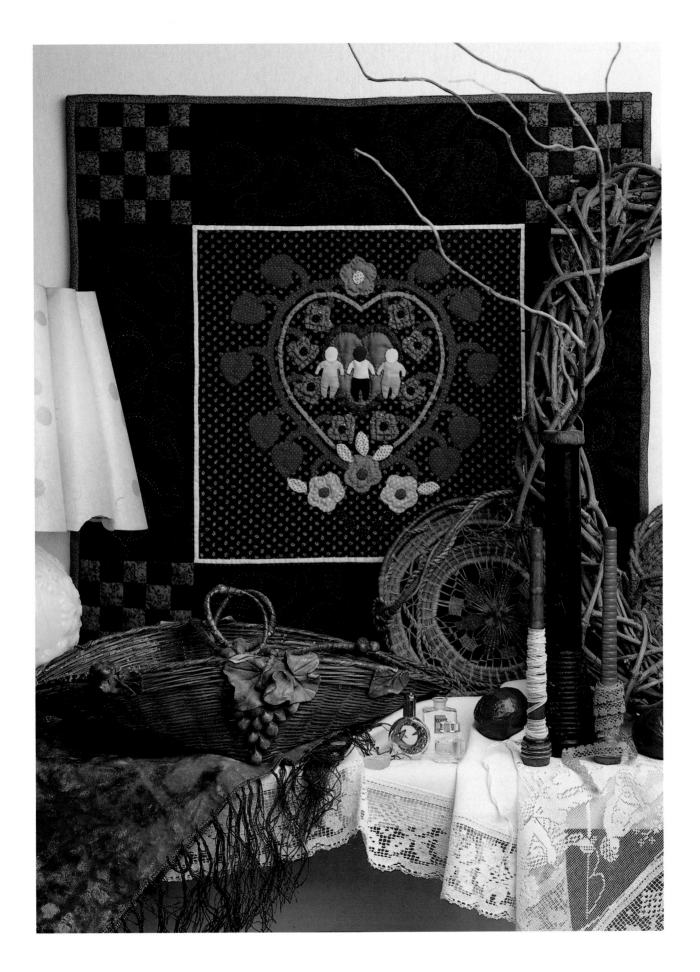

Quilt Top Assembly

Note: Due to the small size of the pieces, seam allowances on all appliqués are ⅛". All other seam allowances are ¼".

1. Appliqué the center block. (Note: Appliqué the design in layers (Diagrams 1-4), completing all work on one layer before proceeding to the next.) Fold 15" dark blue print square in half to locate vertical center fold line. Open square and center heart A on the fold with the bottom point of heart 9½" above bottom edge of square. Baste heart to square. (Do not turn under seam allowances; they will be covered when C is appliquéd.)

Center B around heart A (Diagram 1). Turn under ⅛" seam allowance on B and appliqué to square.

Center C over heart, covering raw edges of A. Turn under seam allowance of C and appliqué to heart (Diagram 2). Add Ds to outer stems of B and appliqué to square. Add E, overlapping the inner stems of B. Appliqué. (Finished width of E should be about ¼".)

Appliqué Fs to inner stems of B (Diagram 3). Appliqué G1s. Appliqué G2s. Cut along dotted lines to make slits at underarm on H pieces. Turn under seam allowances and appliqué as shown in Diagram 3.

Add red pindot J centers to blue flowers, a yellow print J to top blue flower (see photograph), and I centers to green flowers. Add five Is to form a point below the G2s (Diagram 4).

Appliqué a rust K (head) and navy print L (pants) to center figure. Appliqué cream Ks and pink Ls to two outer figures.

Appliqué light yellow print Ms as shown, to add leaves to the three bottom flowers.

2. Add the sashing. Center and stitch one cream strip to one edge of the center block. Repeat for remaining three sides. Miter the corners.

3. Make the checkerboard corner blocks. Join three green strips and two navy strips along long edges, alternating colors. Cut across the band to make twelve 1½"-wide segments. (Note: To prevent unraveling, machine-stitch seams when using this technique.) Repeat with two green strips and three navy strips to piece a band, and cut it into eight 1½"-wide segments.

Join the segments, alternating colors, to make four (5½"-square) checkerboard blocks.

4. Add the border. Join two navy print 5½" x 15½" strips to right and left edges of quilt top. Join checkerboard blocks to ends of the two remaining navy print border pieces. Join strips with checkerboard corners to top and bottom edges of quilt top (Layout and Quilting Schematic).

Quilting

1. Mark the quilting design. Mark the quilting pattern on the navy print border as follows. Place the right-hand edge of the pattern ¼" from the right-hand seam line of one border piece. Mark the pattern. Move the pattern to the left edge of the border and mark the shaded portion again, to complete the design (Diagram 5). Repeat to mark remaining border strips.

Mark the left edge and the top edge of the dark blue print quilt center at 1" intervals. Draw diagonal lines connecting these two sets of dots to create a quilting pattern for the upper left half of the center block (Layout and Quilting Schematic). Use same procedure to mark dots and draw lines for lower right half. Also mark veins inside each D and M (see templates).

2. Stack the layers. Stack the quilt backing (right side down), fleece, and quilt top. Baste securely through all layers, starting at the center and working out to the edge.

3. Quilt. Use yellow thread to quilt around figures in the center, around every appliqué piece, on diagonal lines of the background, on both edges of the sashing, on quilting pattern in border, and along all seams of checkerboard. Also quilt a line down the center of the red pindot heart B, ⅛" inside each F, ⅛" inside each G, and on veins in each D and M.

Trim edges of backing to match quilt top.

Finishing

1. Bind the edges. Join green print bias strips to make a continuous length and use to bind edges of quilt.

Diagram 1

Diagram 2

Diagram 3

Diagram 4

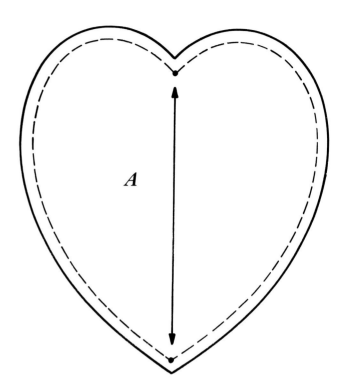

Layout and Quilting Schematic
Note: Dotted lines indicate quilting.

A

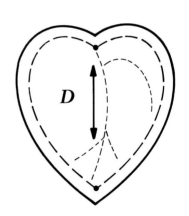

Diagram 5: How to Mark Quilting Pattern

D

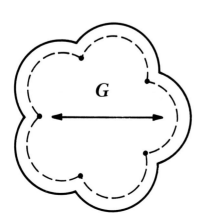

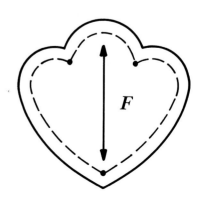

G

F

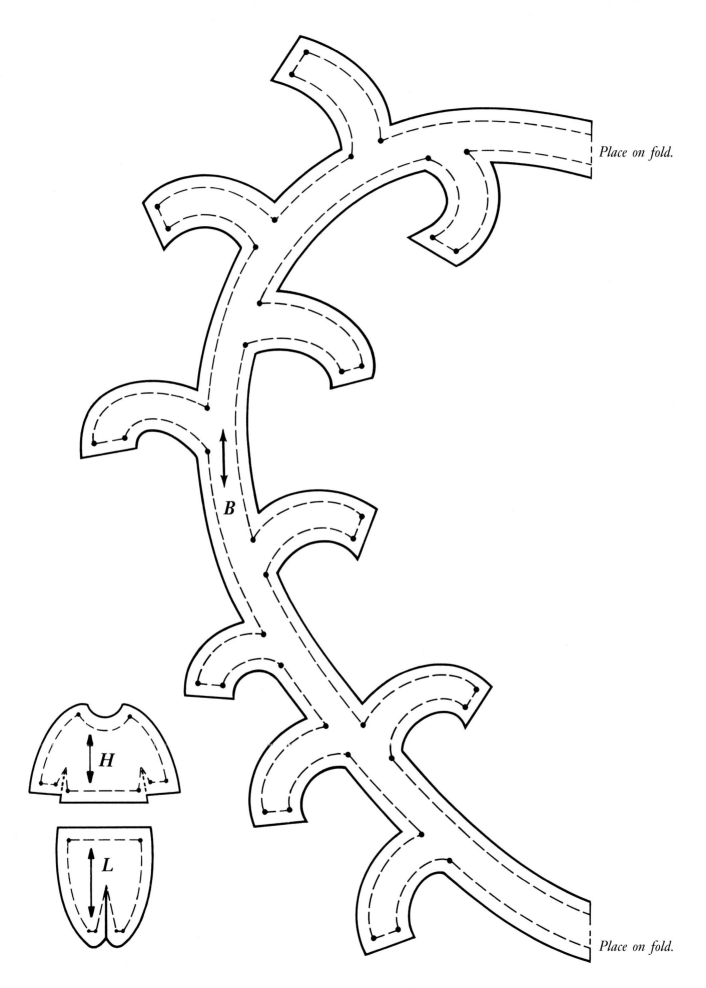

Place on fold.

B

H

L

Place on fold.

140

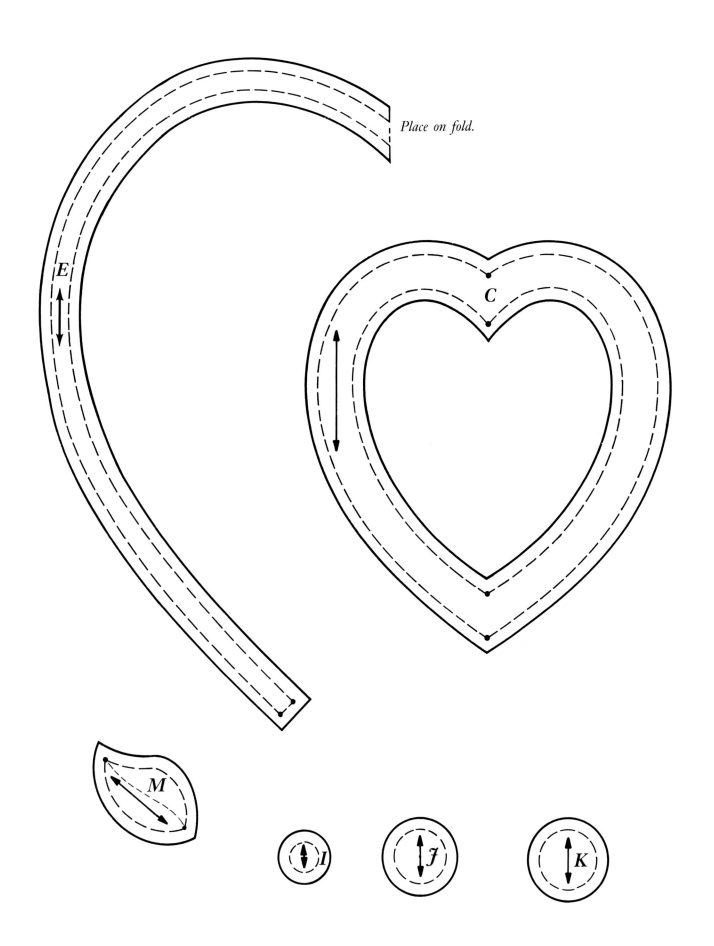

Place on fold.

E

C

M

I

J

K

Clothesline

Many a mother has stitched scraps of her daughter's little dresses into a memory quilt that recalls favorite moments from childhood. But if you can't bear to cut the dresses, display them on this clothesline quilt instead. Pieced in bright, bold hues, the same design would make a fine showcase for a son's first tiny pair of jeans.

Finished size of quilt: *40" x 53"*

Materials

Pink print: *¼ yard*
 Pieces to cut: 30 (template A), 5 (template F), 5 (template F)*

Pink/blue pindot: *½ yard*
 Pieces to cut: 15 (template B), 15 (template B), 15 (template D), 5 (template G), 5 (template G*)*

Pink: *⅛ yard*
 Pieces to cut: 15 (template C), 5 (template H)

Green: *½ yard*
 Pieces to cut: 10 (template E), 10 (template I), 5 (1" x 5") strips for stems

White/green print: *¼ yard*
 Pieces to cut: 5 (template E), 4 (5¼" square)

Muslin: *½ yard*
 Pieces to cut: 5 (template I), 5 (template J), 5 (template K), 4 (template L), 2 (template M),
 4 (template N), 2 (template D)

Pink/cream pindot: *3½ yards*
 Pieces to cut: 1 (24½" x 30½") for clothesline background, 1 (42" x 55") for backing, 5¼ yards of 2"-wide bias strips for binding

Green print: *1¼ yards*
 Pieces to cut: 2 (5¼" x 43½") for border, 2 (5¼" x 30½") for border

Batting: *1½" yards*
 Pieces to cut: 1 (40" x 53")

Cream thread for quilting
Green embroidery floss for feather stitching
1½ yards of ⅜"-wide heavy white trim for clothesline
Six to eight pink rosettes
Baby clothing
Five ⅜"-wide pink/white buttons

Note: *Flip or reverse template if fabric is one-sided.

Quilt Top Assembly
Note: All seam allowances are ¼".

1. Piece the checkerboard rows. Join one pink print A to one pink/blue pindot B. Repeat with A and B* to make the mirror-image A/B* unit (Diagram 1). Join the two units as shown.

Join a pink C to the A/B unit to complete the flower

triangle. Note: Since the two pieces must be joined at a 90° angle, you will get better results if you join the B pieces to the C with separate seams, leaving the two B/B* seam allowances free. Match one C edge to one B edge and join, stitching from corner dot to corner dot without catching the B/B* seam allowances. Flip the B/B* seam allowances out of the way, match the adjacent edge of the C to the B* edge and join as before to complete the flower triangle (you may find it easier to stitch this by hand). Repeat to make 14 more flower triangles. Join each triangle to a D to make 15 small flower squares (Diagram 2).

Join a green E to one small flower square (Diagram 3). Repeat to make four more flower rectangles. Join the completed rectangles as shown (Diagram 4, row 1) to make row 1 of quilt. Repeat to make a second strip (Diagram 4, row 4).

In the same manner, join white/green print Es to remaining small flower squares. Join the completed rectangles as shown (Diagram 4, row 2) to make row 2. Join rows 1 and 2 as shown.

2. Piece the large flower squares. Join one pink print F to one pink/blue G. Repeat with F* and G* to make the mirror-image F*/G* unit (Diagram 5). Join the two units as shown. Join an H to the unit to complete the large flower square. (You may find it easier to stitch H by hand.) Repeat to make four more squares.

To make leaf units, join one muslin I to one green I. Join one muslin J to the I/I unit (Diagram 6) to complete the left leaf unit. For the right leaf unit, join one green I to one muslin K.

Fold a 1"-wide green stem strip in half to make a strip ½"-wide; press. Pin strip to inside edge of right leaf unit, matching raw edges. Join left and right leaf units as shown (Diagram 7). Press folded edge to the right. Turn piece over and trim ends of strip to match edges of leaf units.

To assemble row 3, join five leaf units with four muslin Ls in between. Add a muslin M to each end of strip (see Diagram 4, row 3). Join large flower squares to top edges of leaf strips. Add muslin Ns and Ds to fill in top edge of row 3 as shown. (It may be easier to stitch by hand.) Join row 3 to row 2.

With right sides together, match one 30½" edge of pink/cream pindot rectangle to top edge of row 3. Join. Join row 4 to top edge of pink/cream pindot rectangle to complete the center.

3. Add the border. Stitch 5¼" x 43½" green print strips to right and left edges of the quilt top. Join a white/green 5¼" square to each end of a 5¼" x 30½" green print strip. Repeat to make second border strip. Join border strips to top and bottom edges of quilt top.

Quilting

1. Mark the quilting design. First, mark a diagonal line from the upper left corner of the clothesline section to the center of the right template N in the large flower section (Layout and Quilting Schematic). Then make marks at ¾" intervals across the top edge and left edge of the pink/cream pindot rectangle. Draw lines straight down from the top edge and straight across from the left edge, with lines meeting at the diagonal line. Mark parallel vertical lines to fill in the last 6" of quilting on the right side of the clothesline section.

In each white/green corner block, mark echo-quilting lines ½" apart, ending with a ½"-long horizontal line in the center.

On inside edge of each border piece, mark dots at 1½" intervals along the seam. Draw 45°-angle lines from these points to make a diamond pattern covering the border (see photo).

2. Stack the layers. Stack quilt backing (right side down), batting, and quilt top. Baste securely through all layers.

3. Quilt. Quilt on all marked lines with cream thread. Also quilt in-the-ditch on all seams. Trim backing to match quilt top.

Finishing

1. Bind the edges. Join pink/cream pindot bias strips to make a continuous length and use it to bind edges of quilt.

2. Add the embroidery. Feather-stitch along seam where top meets binding, using two strands of green floss.

3. Position white trim for clothesline. Position trim as shown (see photo) along top edge of pink/cream pindot rectangle. Tack trim at upper corners of rectangle, allowing it to loop down across the mid-section and allowing 10″ extra length to hang free on each end. Fold ends as desired (see photo) and tack. Place baby clothing on quilt (see photo). Secure clothing by tacking rosettes through all layers. Also tack one rosette to each end of clothesline. Sew a button in the center of each template H in tulip section.

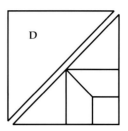

Diagram 2: Small Flower Square

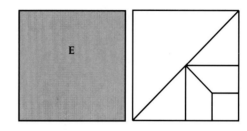

Diagram 3

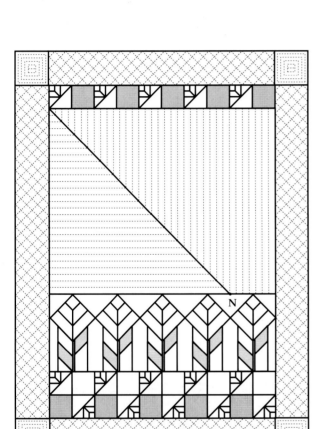

Layout and Quilting Schematic
Note: Dotted lines indicate quilting.

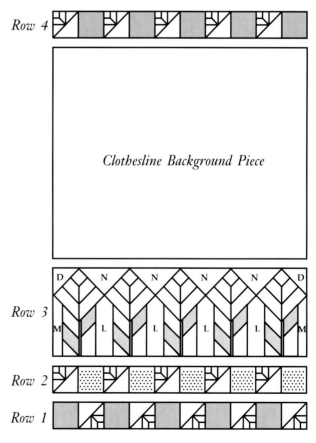

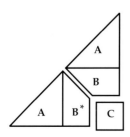

Diagram 1: Flower Triangle

Diagram 4: Assembling Quilt Center

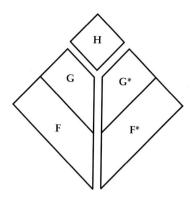

Diagram 5: Large Flower Square

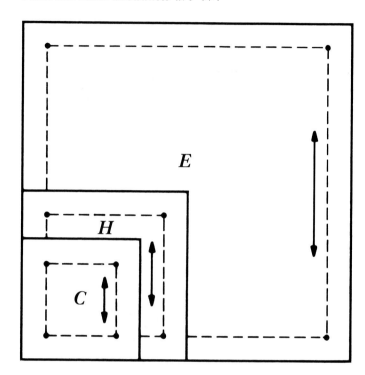

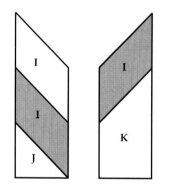

Left leaf unit   Right leaf unit

Diagram 6: Leaf Units

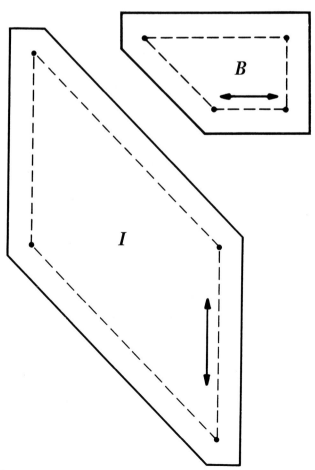

Folded edge

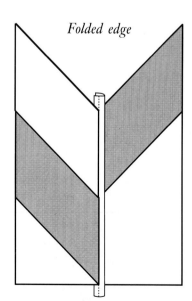

Diagram 7: Inserting Stem Strip

146

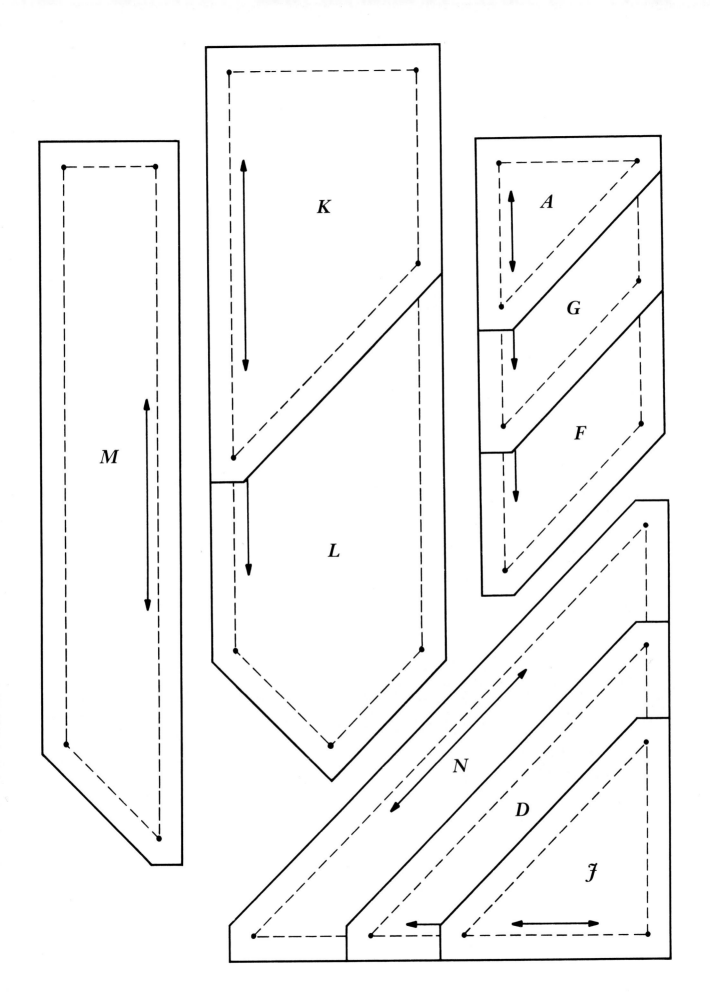

Bunnies in the Garden

*Here's a quilt to win any gardener's heart, a garden in stitches where
the carrots are always sweet, the lettuce is
lush, and the bunnies can nibble to their hearts' content. Since the shapes
are large and simple, even a beginner can
make a great-looking quilt.*

Finished size of quilt: *46" x 46"*

Materials

Dk. green: 3¾ yards
   Pieces to cut: 1 (48" square) for backing, 4 (7½" x 48") for outer border, 4 (4½" x 30") for inner border, 1 (16½" square) for center

Lt. green: ⅝ yard
   Pieces to cut: 5 each (templates B1, B2, B3, B4), 4 each (templates C1, C2)

Apricot: ½ yard
   Pieces to cut: 4 (2" x 48") for border; 12 (template C3)

White: ¼ yard
   Pieces to cut: 4 (template A)

Tan: ¼ yard
   Pieces to cut: 4 (2½" x 30") for border

Polyester fleece: 1½ yards
   Pieces to cut: 1 (46" square), 4 (template A)

Lt. green thread for quilting

Quilt Top Assembly

Note: All seam allowances are ¼".

1. Piece the background. With right sides together, join one 48" dark green strip and one apricot strip along one long edge (Diagram 1). With right sides together, center and join a 30" dark green strip on free edge of apricot strip. With right sides together, join free edge of 30" dark green strip to one edge of one tan strip. Repeat three times to make three more green/apricot, green/tan strips.

With right sides together, center one tan strip on one edge of the 16½" dark green square. Join. Repeat to join border strips to remaining three edges. Miter the corners.

2. Appliqué the rabbits. Trim seam allowance from one fleece A. Pin fleece to wrong side of one rabbit appliqué. Clip curves and turn under seam allowance of fabric. Appliqué rabbit to quilt top (Layout and Quilting Schematic). Repeat for remaining rabbits. (Notice that one rabbit is reversed.)

3. Appliqué the lettuce. Turn under seam allowances and appliqué lettuce pieces onto quilt top (Diagram 2).

4. Appliqué the carrots. Turn under seam allowance and appliqué carrot pieces onto quilt top (Diagram 3).

Quilting

1. Mark the quilting design. Mark diagonal quilting lines 2" apart on dark green outer border and center square (Layout and Quilting Schematic). Also mark

quilting lines on carrots and lettuce (refer to dotted lines on patterns).

2. Stack the layers. Stack the quilt backing (right side down), fleece, and quilt top. Baste securely through all layers.

3. Quilt. Quilt on all marked lines and around each appliquéd piece, using light green thread.

Finishing

1. Make self-binding. Fold the excess fabric from the quilt backing to the front. Turn under the raw edge and slipstitch to front to make a ½"-wide self-binding.

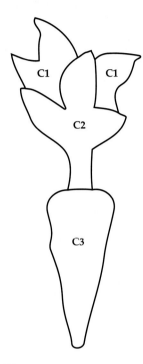

Diagram 3: Placement of Carrot Templates

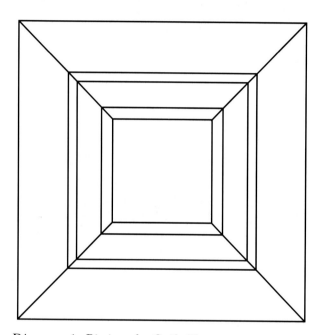

Diagram 1: Piecing the Quilt Top

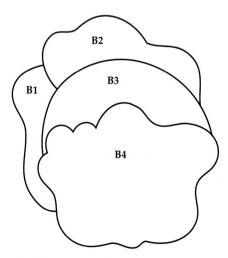

Diagram 2: Placement of Lettuce Templates

Layout and Quilting Schematic
Note: Dotted lines indicate quilting.

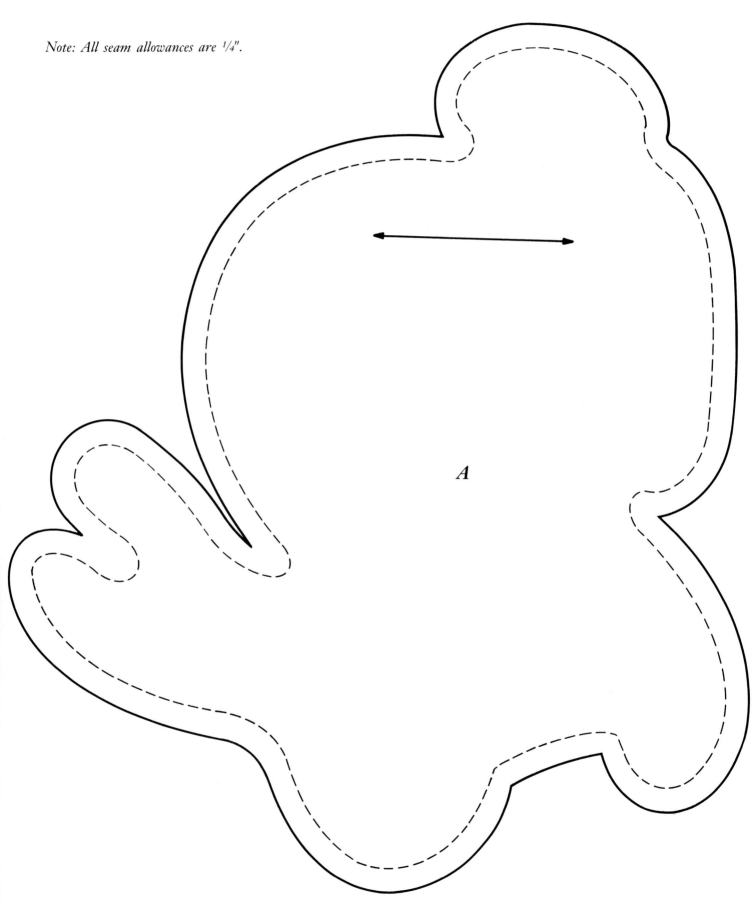

A

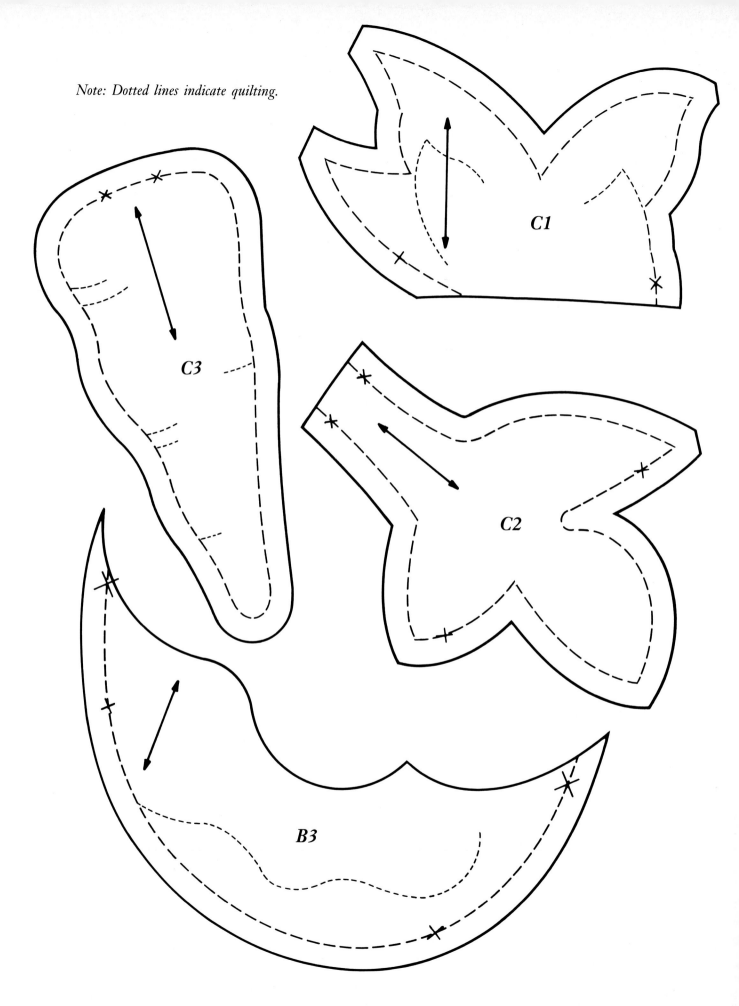

Note: Dotted lines indicate quilting.

C1

C3

C2

B3

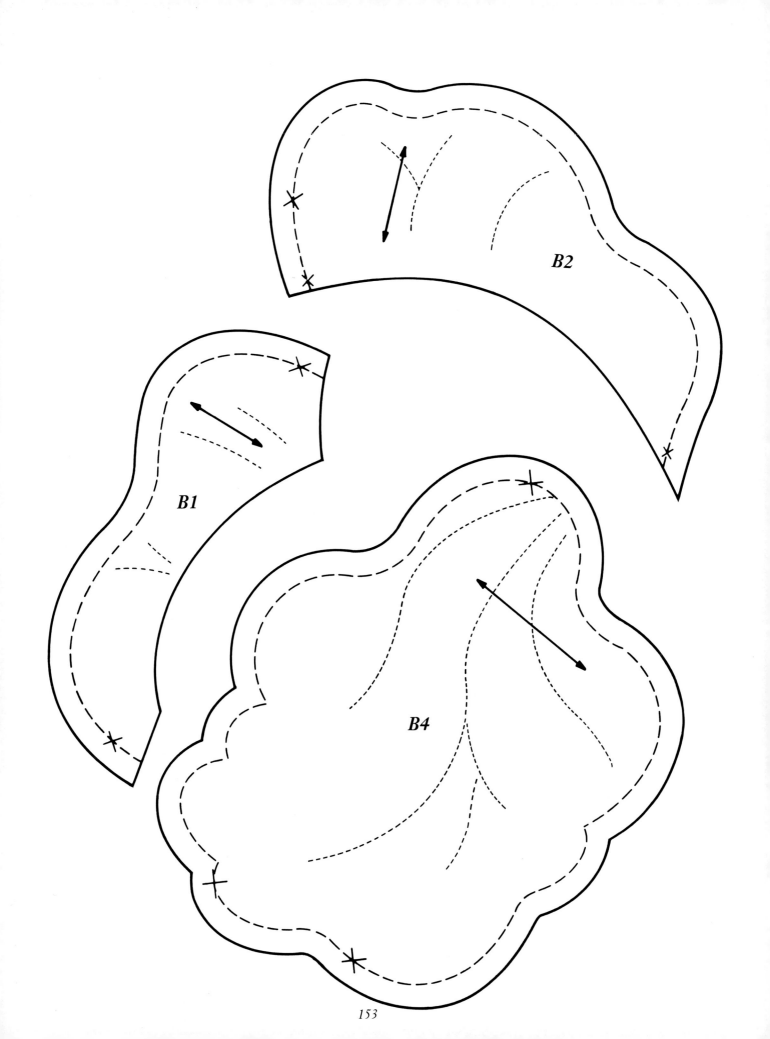

B2

B1

B4

Appendix

Preliminary Instructions

All templates include ¼″ seam allowances unless otherwise noted. Measurements given for backing, sashing strips, border strips, and other pieces also include ¼″ seam allowances.

Measurements for quilt backings are 2″ longer and wider than the desired finished size, to allow for adjustment if layers should shift during quilting. Border strips that will be mitered at each end are cut 2″ longer than desired finished length, to allow for adjustment at the corners if needed.

Fabric requirements are based on 44″/45″-wide fabric with trimmed selvages and include a generous amount to allow for shrinkage and differences in layout. The yardage recommendations are figured to allow border strips to be cut in one piece and bias strips to be cut in continuous lengths of at least one yard.

Finished quilt size is the size of the quilt before quilting.

Making Templates

Make templates from clear quilters' vinyl or cardboard.

If using vinyl, place it over each pattern piece and carefully copy cutting lines, stitching lines, grain lines (arrows), and corner dots with an indelible marker. Label each piece with pattern name and letter. Punch holes at corner dots, using a ⅛″ hole punch. Cut along the cutting line to separate pieces.

For cardboard templates, use dressmakers' carbon paper to transfer pattern markings to cardboard. Place the carbon paper between the pattern and the cardboard, carefully copy all markings, and cut out as above.

Preparation and Marking of Fabric

Wash, dry, and press all fabrics before marking and cutting.

Use a #2 pencil, a dressmakers' pencil, or a water-soluble marker to trace templates on light-colored fabric for cutting. Use an artists' pastel pencil, dressmakers' pencil, or sliver of soap for dark fabrics. (To make sure markings will come out, mark a scrap of fabric, wash it, and dry it, before tracing templates onto quilt fabric.)

Practice positioning and tracing pattern pieces on graph paper to determine an economical layout; then lay them out on fabric. Unless otherwise specified, mark on the wrong side of the fabric (except for appliqués, which are always traced on the right side).

Align grain lines on template with lengthwise grain of fabric (parallel to the selvage). Trace around template to mark cutting line; then mark corner dots. If desired, mark stitching line as well.

Use a ruler to mark cutting lines for border and sashing strips, backing fabric, and other pieces for which no templates are given. (Align longest edge of each piece with the lengthwise or crosswise grain.)

If bias strips are required for binding or appliqués, to conserve fabric, mark these strips first. With the aid of a yardstick, mark the strips on the bias of the fabric, at a 45° angle to the selvage. Lay out template pieces and other pieces to be cut on either side of the bias strips.

Cut out all pieces with sharp dressmakers' scissors or a rotary cutter, cutting right on the cutting line.

Piecing

The explosion diagrams that accompany many of the

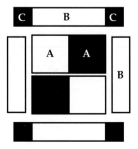

Diagram 1

quilts show you the most efficient sequence for piecing the blocks.

The amount of space between units on an explosion diagram indicates the order in which the units should be joined (Diagram 1). First, sew together any units that are shown joined (no spaces between units) on the diagram. Units with the narrowest space between them should be joined next. Progressively wider spaces indicate progressively later steps in assembly.

To prepare two units for joining, place pieces with right sides together, matching the pieces along seam lines and securing them with pins at corner dots. Where two seams meet along a third seam line (Diagram 2), press seam allowances in opposite directions to reduce bulk and secure with a pin. Use additional pins along the seam line as needed.

Diagram 2

To join units by machine, stitch along the seam line, using about 12 stitches per inch and removing pins as you come to them. Press seam allowances to one side. For best results, press as you go. Always press each seam before crossing it with another.

To join units by hand, use a small embroidery or quilting needle and a single strand of thread. Knot the thread and begin by taking a small backstitch at the beginning of the seam. Stitch along the seam line with small, even running stitches (about 8 to 10 stitches per inch). At the end of the seam, take a small backstitch to secure the thread, run the needle through the backstitch, and pull tight to knot thread.

Appliqué

All appliqué quilts in this book were stitched by hand. To cut and mark pieces for hand appliqué, you will need two kinds of templates: standard cutting templates marked with both cutting and stitching lines (for marking fabric pieces to be cut) and finished-size templates (made by cutting away the seam allowances) to

mark the fold line for the appliqués and to mark positions of appliqués on the quilt.

There are a number of methods for hand appliqué. Experiment with scraps of fabric to find the method that works best for you.

The simplest way is to pin the pieces in place on the background fabric, baste them to secure, and then, turning the seam allowance under as you go, slipstitch the folded edge to the backing.

To hold pieces in place, baste ½" from the raw edge if the seam allowance is ¼"; ¼" from the raw edge if the seam allowance is ⅛". As you appliqué, turn under the seam allowance 1" to 2" ahead of where you are stitching, creasing the fold line with your fingers. To make the edge lie flat around inside curves, clip the seam allowance almost to the fold line where needed. Clip excess fabric from tips of corners to eliminate bulk.

Slipstitch the appliqué to the background fabric with matching thread, using tiny, even stitches that are ⅛" apart on straight edges and even closer around inside curves and sharp points.

To allow extra control and to reinforce areas to be clipped, you may prefer to machine-stitch around each appliqué cutout first, just outside the marked stitching line. Use the line of stitching as a guide to fold under the seam allowance. (Press or baste folded edge before attaching appliqué to background fabric.)

Positioning the appliqués is less critical on simple designs such as *Bunnies in the Garden* and *Cow in the Clover*. But for more intricate designs, such as *Warm-hearted Snowflake*, you may want to lightly trace the outline of each piece on the background in the proper position, using a finished-size template. Then use the traced lines as a guide for placement and appliqué.

Mitering Corners

The crisp lines of mitered corners add a professional finish to borders and blocks and require only a little extra effort. To ensure perfect mitered corners, begin by folding each border strip widthwise to find its center. Mark the center with a dot. Then center and mark the exact desired length of the seam line on the strip with a dot at each end (called a corner dot). Match the center and the corner dots of strips to center and corner dots of quilt edges and join. (Note: Stitch only between corner dots: do not allow the stitching to extend into the seam allowance.)

With quilt right side up, begin at lower right corner and lap the bottom border strip over the side border strip as shown (Diagram 3). Draw a diagonal line connecting the upper left corner of the lap to the lower right corner (dotted line on diagram).

Turn under bottom border on the marked line and iron the fold (Diagram 4). Fold under the side border so that the two diagonal folds meet exactly. Iron the second fold.

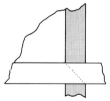

Diagram 3

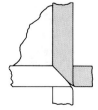

Diagram 4

With right sides of the two border strips together, match and pin the two ironed fold lines together. Join the pieces along the fold line. Trim seam allowances to ¼″ and press seam open. Repeat for remaining corners.

Quilting

When the top is completed, mark the quilting design, using the method you selected for marking templates above. Then stack backing (right side down), batting or fleece, and the marked quilt top, centering the batting and then the top on the backing. Starting at the center of the quilt and working out, pin and then baste through all layers to secure.

All the quilts in this book were quilted by hand. For best results, use quilting thread and a small embroidery or quilting needle. Most quilters prefer to hide their beginning and ending knots by burying them in the quilt batting. Insert needle in backing and bring it out on the top of the quilt. Gently tug at the thread until the knot pops through the fabric and lodges in the batting. Quilt through all layers with small, evenly spaced running stitches (7 or 8 stitches per inch is a nice goal to work toward).

To fasten off, bring the needle out on the top of the quilt. Take a tiny backstitch on the quilt top, right where the thread comes out, run the needle through the backstitch loop, and pull the thread tight to form a knot. Plunge the needle into the quilt top at the knot and exit on the top side, about 1″ away. Pull the thread tight to pop the knot into the batting; then clip off the excess length.

Binding

When quilting is completed, the raw edges of a quilt must be covered to give the quilt a finished look and protect the edges from wear. Bias binding is a popular choice because it is easier to smooth around corners and curves and can be purchased ready-made. But binding cut on the straight grain also works well, especially if the edges of the quilt are straight and the binding is mitered at the corners.

Place binding on quilt top with right sides together, matching raw edges. Join. Fold binding to wrong side of quilt, covering raw edge. Fold under ¼″ seam allowance on binding and slipstitch folded edge to quilt back (Diagram 5).

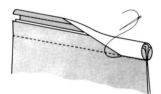

Diagram 5

A double layer of binding may be used for double protection. Cut it twice as wide as single binding, minus ½″. Fold the binding in half lengthwise to double it and sew it to the right side of the quilt, with folded edge facing toward center of quilt. Fold binding over the raw edge of the quilt and slipstitch the folded edge to the backing.

The Finishing Touch

Always sign and date your work, to add to its value and to enrich its meaning for future generations.

The simplest way to do this is to write your name and the date with indelible fabric marker on a scrap of well-washed fabric and neatly sew the scrap to the back of the quilt.

For a signature that is guaranteed to weather the test of time (and endless washings), take a few extra minutes to embroider it. Stitch along the letters with a single line of stem stitch, chain stitch, or backstitch, using embroidery floss that complements the color of the backing. Or work the lettering out on graph paper and cross-stitch your signature instead.

Anatomy of a Quilt

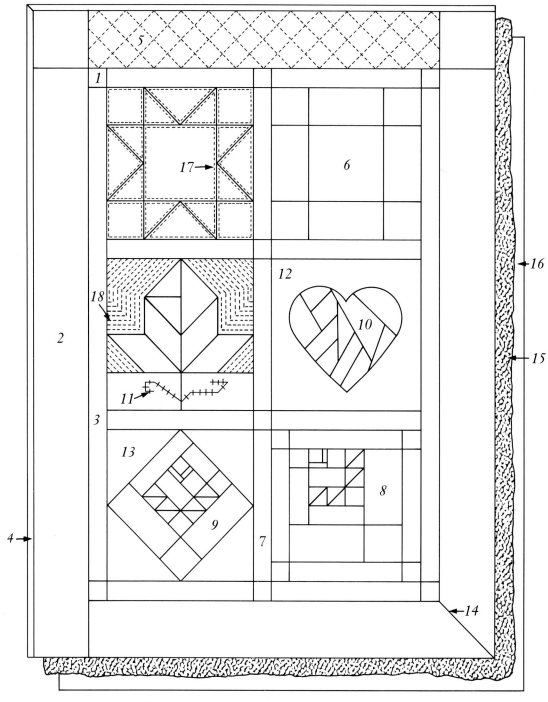

1. Corner Square
2. Outside Border
3. Inside Border
4. Binding
5. Quilting

6. Pieced Block
7. Sashing
8. Straight Setting
9. On-Point Setting
10. Crazy Patch

11. Embroidered Detail
12. Appliquéd Block
13. Corner Triangle
14. Mitered Corner
15. Batting

16. Backing
17. Outline Quilting
18. Echo Quilting

Glossary

APPLIQUÉ: A design made by cutting shapes from fabric and applying them by hand or machine to another piece of fabric.

BACKING: The fabric that forms the bottom or back layer of the quilt.

BACKSTITCH: A stitch in which the thread moves one stitch length backward on the right side of the fabric and then two stitch lengths forward on the wrong side. Short backstitches are used by quilters to secure stitches at the beginning or end of a line of hand stitching. Backstitching can be used instead of knots to anchor a thread or inserted at regular intervals to strengthen a line of running stitch.

BASTING STITCHES: Long running stitches used to hold two or more layers of fabric in place while quilting. Baste with a single strand of white thread. (Basting stitches are temporary, to be removed when quilting is finished.)

BATTING (sometimes called a batt): Layers or sheets of fibrous material used as a filler between the quilt top and the backing. Batting provides thickness and warmth. Polyester batting should be bonded by the manufacturer to prevent shifting of the fibers during quilting and laundering.

BIAS: A line diagonal to the grain of a woven fabric. Fabric cut on the bias has much greater elasticity than fabric cut on the lengthwise or crosswise grain. This characteristic should be taken into account when laying out quilt pieces.

BINDING: A narrow folded strip of fabric used to enclose the raw outside edges of the quilt or to make narrow strips for appliqué. Binding is usually cut on the bias, but is occasionally cut on the straight grain.

BLOCK: A unit of patchwork or appliqué, usually in the form of a square, which is often repeated to construct an entire quilt top.

BORDER: Plain, pieced, or appliquéd bands of fabric, used to frame the central section of the quilt top.

CRAZY PATCH: A type of patchwork in which odd shapes of fabric are appliquéd to a foundation block in a random design. Embroidery stitches are often used to accent seams. (*Crazy Hearts* quilt is a good example.)

ECHO-QUILT: To repeat a quilting line in equally spaced rows, parallel to a seam or to the edge of an appliquéd piece. (See corner squares on *Clothesline* for a good example.)

FLEECE: A soft, felt-like polyester interfacing fabric that can be substituted for batting in quilts when a flatter, less puffy effect is preferred.

GRAIN: The direction in which the threads of a fabric are woven. The lengthwise grain of the fabric runs parallel to the selvage edges. (This grain has the least amount of stretch.) The crosswise grain runs perpendicular to the selvage edges and has a little more stretch than the lengthwise grain.

GRID: A network of uniformly spaced squares, often used as a quilting pattern.

HAND QUILTING: Small running stitches made through all layers to hold the top, batting, and backing of the quilt together.

MACHINE QUILTING: Quilting stitched on a sewing machine.

MITER: Joining vertical and horizontal strips of fabric at a 45° angle to form a 90° corner. (Mitered corners are often used in constructing borders.)

ON POINT: A quilt square with the diagonal oriented in a vertical direction (a square standing on its corner or point).

OUTLINE QUILTING: A single row of quilting

stitched parallel to the pieced or appliquéd seam lines of a quilt. Outline quilting is traditionally worked far enough from the seam line to fall just outside the seam allowances, to make the stitching easier.

PIECING/PIECED BLOCK: Pieces of fabric cut in desired shapes and sewn together to produce a pattern, often producing a square.

QUILTING IN-THE-DITCH: Quilting as close as possible to the seam line on the side opposite the seam allowances.

QUILTING/QUILTING STITCHES: Stitches used to secure the three layers of the quilt together, often arranged in a decorative pattern. The quilting can be done either by hand or machine.

QUILT TOP: The decorative layer of the quilt. It can be pieced, appliquéd, or a combination of the two.

REVERSE APPLIQUÉ: A decorative technique in which holes are cut in the top layer of a fabric to reveal the layer underneath. Edges of the opening are turned under and slipstitched to the background fabric to complete the reverse appliqué.

RUNNING STITCH: A line of short, even stitches used for hand piecing and quilting.

SASHING: Strips of fabric used to join block to block.

SEAM ALLOWANCE: The distance between the cut edge of fabric and the stitching line. In quilt making, this is usually 1/4". However, if the pieces of the quilt are small, 1/4" seam allowances may overlap on the back

when the quilt is assembled, causing excess bulk. If this occurs, trim the seam allowances to 1/8".

SELVAGES: The lengthwise finished edges on each side of woven fabric.

SLIPSTITCH: A small, almost invisible stitch used to secure a folded edge to a flat surface. Use a single strand of thread with a knot tied in one end.

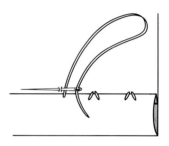

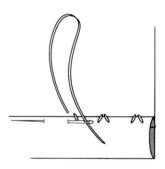

STACKING: The process of layering the quilt backing, the batting, and the quilt top in preparation for quilting.

TEMPLATE: A copy of a pattern unit, made from cardboard, plastic, or sandpaper.